The Sting of the *Hawke*

Collision in the Solent

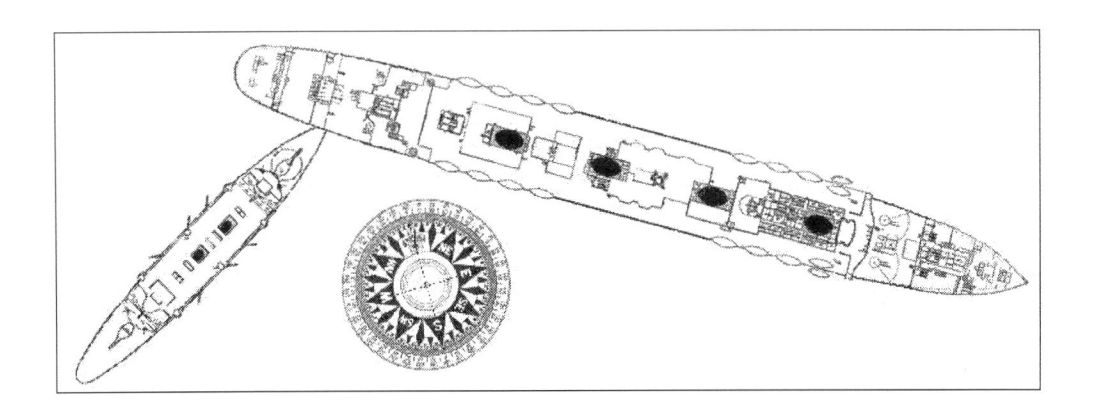

Samuel Halpern

and

Mark Chirnside

The Full Story Behind the Collision Between
HMS *Hawke* and RMS *Olympic* on 20 September 1911

Copyright © 2014 by Samuel Halpern and Mark Chirnside

All rights reserved. This book or any portion thereof
may not be reproduced or used in any manner whatsoever
without the express written permission of the authors.

ISBN-13: 978-1502946874
ISBN-10: 1502946874

About the authors:

Samuel Halpern is a systems engineer and technologist by profession, with a longstanding interest in steamships and sailing vessels, the study of naval architecture and the practice of celestial and coastal navigation. He has been involved with the study of *Titanic* for many years, and is the principal author of the book *Report Into the Loss of the SS Titanic – A Centennial Reappraisal* (The History Press, 2011). Sam has also written numerous research articles for the Titanic Historical Society's *The Titanic Commutator*, the British Titanic Society's *Atlantic Daily Bulletin*, the Irish Titanic Historical Society's *White Star Journal* and the Titanic International Society's *Voyage* as well as publishing a number of online articles at *Encyclopedia Titanica*, *Great Lakes Titanic Society*, *Titanic Research and Modeling Association*, *Mark Chirnside's Reception Room* and on his own *Titanicology* website. In addition to *Titanic*, Sam has conducted an in-depth analysis and report into the 1956 collision between *Stockholm* and *Andrea Doria* that was presented at the Maine Maritime Academy and is also available on his *Titanicology* website. He also holds a private pilot's certificate for single-engine land aircraft, and was a yachtsman's mate on a Catalina 25 in the 1980s, spending many weekends cruising the waters off Staten Island, Sandy Hook and Lower New York Bay.

Mark Chirnside is an accomplished researcher and historian. He has authored a number of books about *Olympic*, *Titanic* and *Britannic* and several other vessels including *Aquitania*, *Majestic* and others. He is one of several co-authors of the book *Report Into the Loss of the SS Titanic – A Centennial Reappraisal* (The History Press, 2011). Mark's book, *The 'Olympic' Class Ships* (The History Press, 2011), is a revised and expanded edition of a detailed and original history of *Olympic* and her two sister ships *Titanic* and *Britannic*. When it first came out, it won "Ships Monthly's" Book of the Month, the first of three such awards for his books. Mark's most recent book, *RMS Olympic: Titanic's Sister* (The History Press, 2015), is a revised and expanded edition of his detailed *Olympic* history, which was first published in 2004. Mark also has written numerous articles for various journals, such as the British Titanic Society's *Atlantic Daily Bulletin*, the Titanic Historical Society's *The Titanic Commutator*, the Irish Titanic Historical Society's *White Star Journal* and the Titanic International Society's *Voyage*. His website, *Mark Chirnside's Reception Room*, contains a wealth of information with links to many of his articles and papers.

CONTENTS

Preface	Page 1
Prologue	Page 10
Chapter 1. "There's Going to be a Collision"	Page 12
Chapter 2. A One-Sided Enquiry	Page 23
Chapter 3. Trial in the High Court of Justice	Page 27
Chapter 4. Appeals and Judgments	Page 35
Chapter 5. An *Olympic* Tale	Page 42
Chapter 6. A *Hawke*'s Tale	Page 54
Chapter 7. In Search of Reality	Page 65
Chapter 8. Damages and Repairs	Page 84
Chapter 9. Causes and Alternatives	Page 91
Chapter 10. Incident at Southampton	Page 97
Epilogue	Page 101
Appendix A. Hydrodynamic Forces and Interactions	Page 103
Appendix B. The Equation of Continuity	Page 108
Acknowledgements	Page 110
Index	Page 111

PREFACE

Samuel Halpern

This book deals with the collision between HMS *Hawke* and RMS *Olympic* that occurred in the Solent back in September 1911. As with any account that deals with maritime matters, much use is made of terms and phrases that may be somewhat unfamiliar to the non-nautical minded person. Furthermore, some terms and phrases used in 1911 differed from those that are used today. So the reader can best understand what is being presented here, some of the most often used terms and phrases are defined in this section.

The following diagram (Fig. P-01), using RMS *Olympic* as an example, is presented so the reader can become familiar with some of the more important shipboard locations and relative directions that were referred to during the enquiry and court proceedings that followed the collision between HMS *Hawke* and RMS *Olympic* back in 1911.

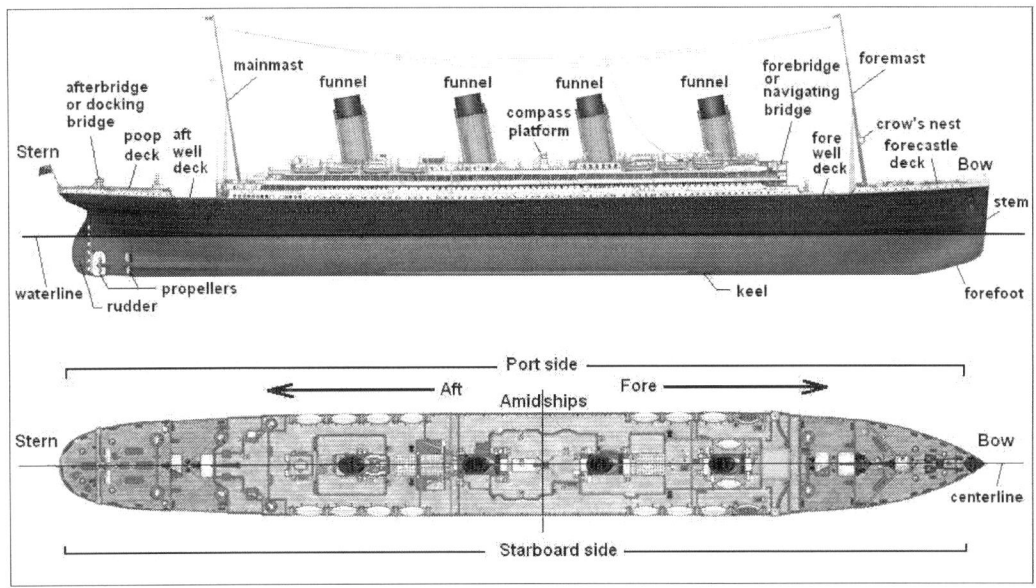

Fig. P-01 RMS *Olympic* in 1911.

Angular Directions and Compass Points

Many references were made in the enquiries to angular directions, both magnetic and relative. When a ship's heading was given it usually was in degrees as marked on a compass, either the ship's standard compass or a steering compass. On *Olympic*, the standard compass was mounted on a platform that was located amidships on the ship's centerline. On HMS *Hawke*, the standard compass was located on the roof of the bridge over the chartroom on the ship's centerline. Not only was the standard compass used to steady a ship on a desired magnetic courseline, but it also served to take magnetic bearings of celestial objects and landmarks when needed. The steering compass was the compass by which the helmsman, the man at the wheel, used to steer the ship.

Because magnetic compasses are affected by the distribution of iron and steel within a ship, they are subjected to errors know as deviation errors which varied with the actual magnetic heading that the ship was on at a given time. These deviation errors were tested and somewhat compensated for when a compass was last adjusted. Typically, the remaining deviation error was only a few degrees, and was marked in a table or on a diagram that gave the deviation error in terms of degrees to be added or subtracted from the ship's heading that was read on the compass card.

Because the axis of the earth's magnetic poles are not aligned exactly with the earth's axis of rotation, the direction of true north typically differs from the direction of magnetic north, depending on where you are on the earth's surface. This difference is known as magnetic variation. In the Solent in September 1911, magnetic variation was 15° 57' west. What that means is that north on a magnetic compass displaying zero deviation error (like one mounted on a wooden sailboat) would actually be pointing about 16 degrees west of true north as shown below.

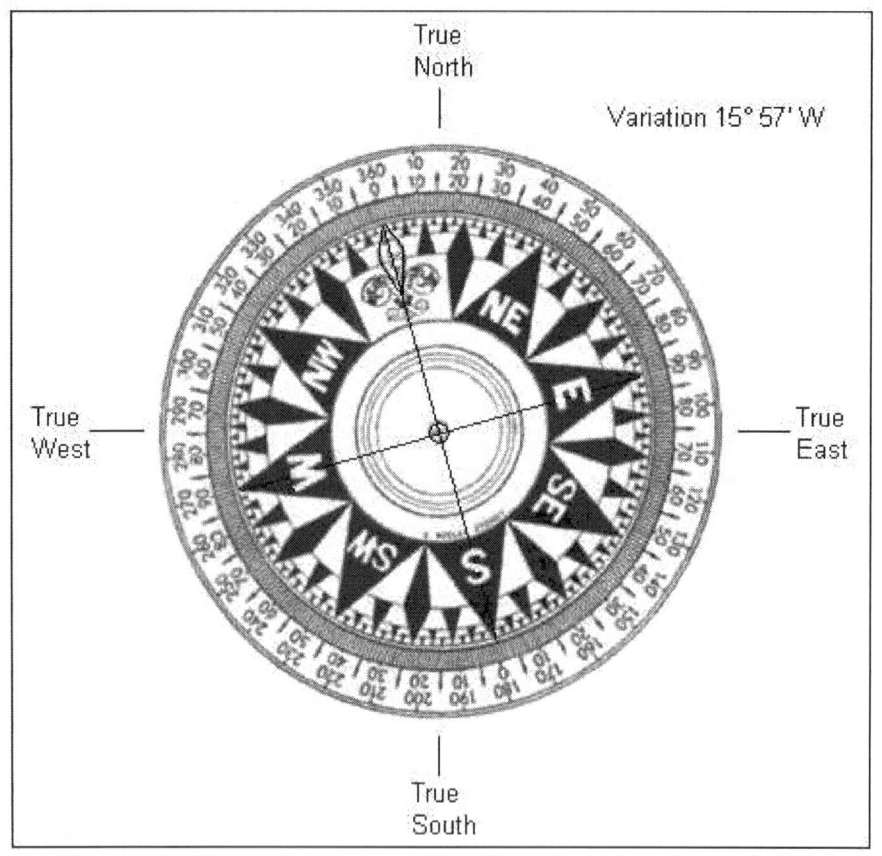

Fig. P-02 Magnetic Compass Showing Variation of 15° 57' W.

The compass rose shown in the above diagram (Fig. P-02) has three scales. The outermost scale is marked in degrees measured clockwise from north (indicated by a crown symbol) through 360. Just inside of that is a scale showing degrees by quadrant; 0 through 90 measured from N to E for the northeastern quadrant, 0 through 90 measured from south to east for the southeastern quadrant, 0 through 90 measured from south to west for the southwestern quadrant, and 0 through 90 measured from north to west for the northwestern quadrant. The innermost scale shows angular directions in points.

In all, there are 32 points in a circle, with each point precisely separated by 11 ¼ degrees from the next point. Included in the set of 32 points are the four cardinal points, north (N), east (E), south (S), and west (W); four intercardinal points, northeast (NE), southeast (SE), southwest (SW), and northwest (NW); and eight secondary-intercardinal points such as north-northeast (NNE), east-northeast (ENE), east-southeast (ESE), and so on. These secondary-intercardinal points are located between each cardinal and inter-cardinal point. In the compass rose above, marks (in the shape of triangles of various sizes) for every point, ½ point and ¼ point can be seen.

In modern times, courses are specified in 360-degree notation by three digits. For example, a ship heading due east true is said to be on a course heading of 090° T. With 16° west variation, the ship's magnetic heading would be specified as 106° magnetic. In 1911, the magnetic compass was marked in degrees by quadrant and by points. Therefore a ship that was steadied onto a course of 106° magnetic would be said to be heading S 74° E magnetic.

A typical compass card of the period is shown in Figure P-03 below.

Fig. P-03   Compass card circa 1911.

Angular directions to objects were specified by bearings, either compass bearings or relative bearings. If a compass bearing was specified, it usually was given by reference to points. For example, an object sighted ½ point to the west of the northwest (NW) intercardinal point on the compass would be said to be bearing NW ½ W. If sighted 1 point to the west of NW, it would be said to be bearing NW by W. If sighted 1 ½ points to the west of NW, it would be said to be bearing NW by W ½ W. And if sighted 2 points to the west of NW, it would be bearing on the secondary-intercardinal point of west-northwest (WNW). Similarly for other points of the compass.

If the angle to an object was specified by a relative bearing, it would be given in relation to the head of one's own vessel. Unlike today, where relative bearings are specific in degrees from the head of the vessel to the object, relative bearings back then were almost always specified in points. For example, an object sighted exactly 22 ½ degrees to the right of the direction that the ship's bow was facing would be said to be "2 points on the starboard bow." An object sighted 45 degrees to the left of the direction that the ship's stern was facing would be said to be "4 points on the starboard quarter" or "broad on the starboard quarter."

The diagram below (Fig. P-04) shows the relative bearings in 1 point increments that were used at the time.

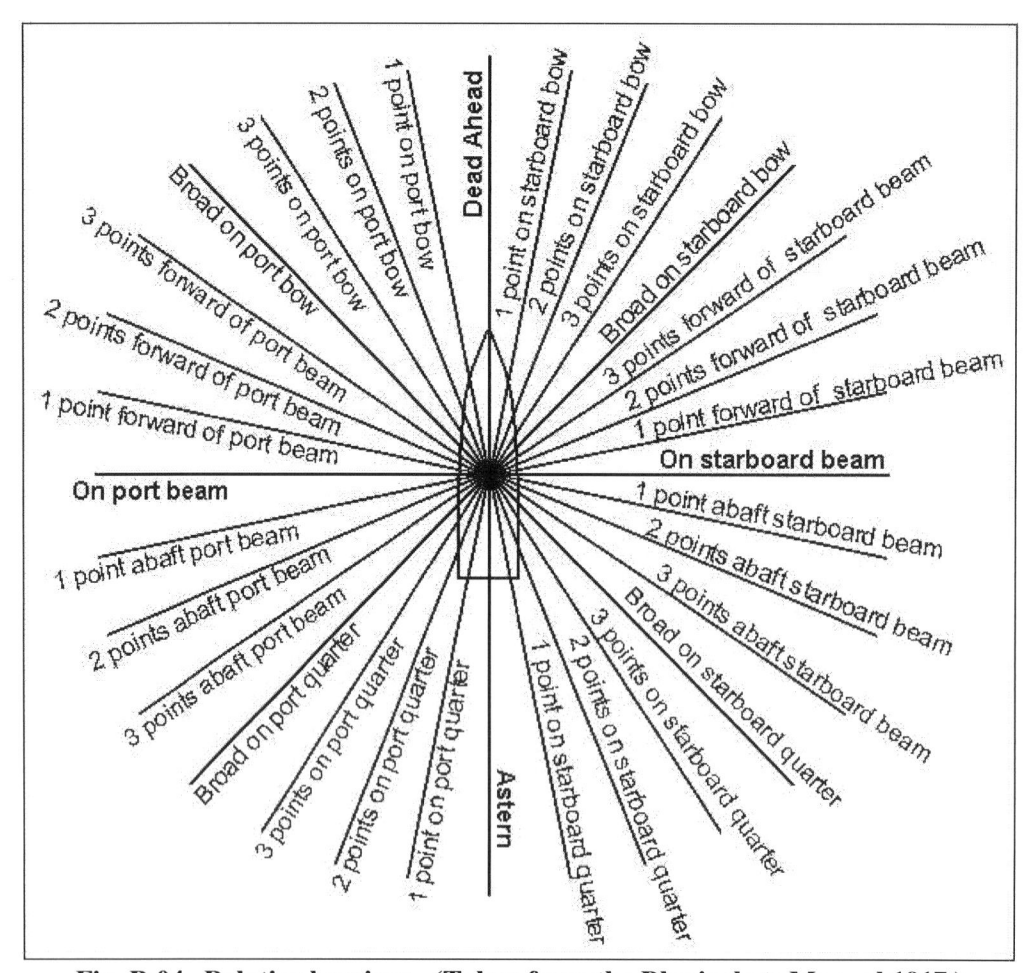

Fig. P-04 Relative bearings. (Taken from the Bluejackets Manual 1917.)

Helm Orders and Turning Directions

One area of great confusion to many people already familiar with most nautical terms has to do with helm orders. In 1911 helm orders were the same as that which came down from the days of sail. On a sailing vessel if one wanted to turn the vessel's head to port (to the left) the tiller had to be put over to starboard (to the right). Thus the order would be given to starboard the helm. The tiller was firmly attached to the rudder post, and putting the tiller over to starboard would throw the rudder, which pointed aft, over to port. With the rudder over to port, the action of water running past it would create a force on the rudder that would cause the vessel's stern to swing out in the opposite direction over to starboard. This in turn would cause the vessel's head to turn to port, and the vessel would begin to turn in a circle to the left. Even when the steering gear was controlled by a wheel, to turn the vessel's head to port the order would be given to put the helm, and thus the vessel's tiller, over to starboard. To do this, the helmsman would turn the wheel to the left in a counter-clockwise direction. The opposite would apply to turn a vessel in the opposite direction.

It was not just helm orders that reflected terminology that came down from the days of sail. When a vessel was seen turning to port (to the left), it was described as being "starboarded." Think of it as describing the direction in which the vessel's stern was swinging as a vessel was being turned. Similarly, if the vessel was seen turning to starboard (to the right), it would be described as being "ported." The diagram below (Fig. P-05) shows all this.

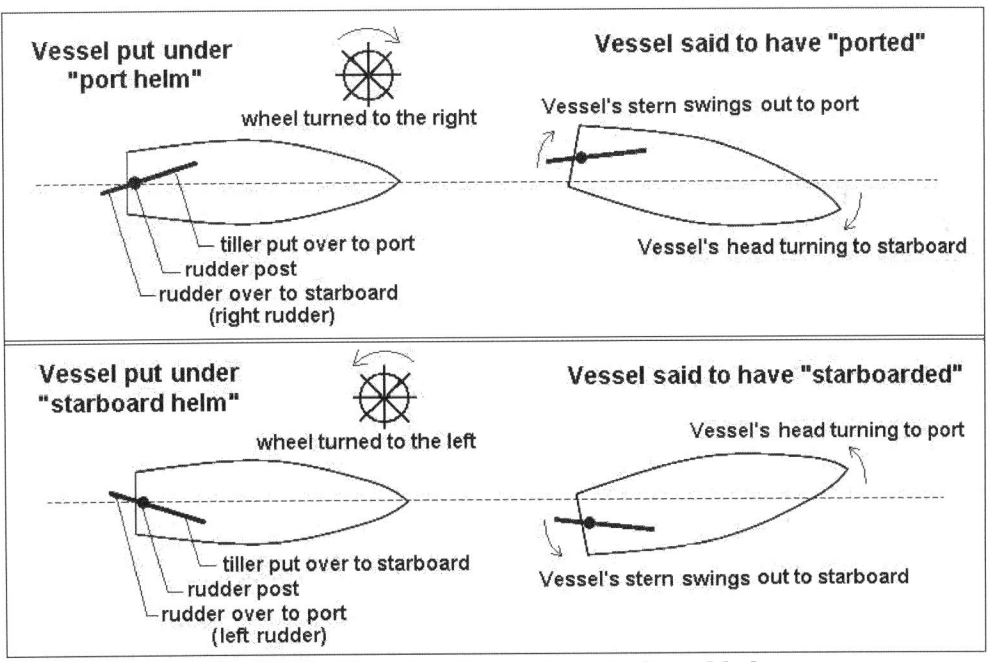

Fig. P-05   Vessel under port or starboard helm.

The following diagram (Fig. P-06) shows a typical steering gear arrangement used on steamships in the early 20th century. Unlike the rope-and-tiller steering arrangement used in large sailing ships, where tiller ropes and pulleys connected the ship's tiller directly to the ship's wheel, steamships needed something much more powerful to control their massive rudders. Thus the mechanism by which the rudder and its attached tiller were actually worked was by means of a steering quadrant driven by a steam engine located under the poop. This steam engine, called a steering engine, was controlled by means of a hydraulic telemotor that was connected to the wheel on the navigating bridge or in a wheelhouse. The outer arms of the steering quadrant were connected loosely to a hub that rotated freely on the rudder post. The ship's working tiller, located between these outer arms, was keyed solidly to the rudder post and was linked to the outer arms of the quadrant by heavy springs to absorb any shocks that may act on the rudder itself.

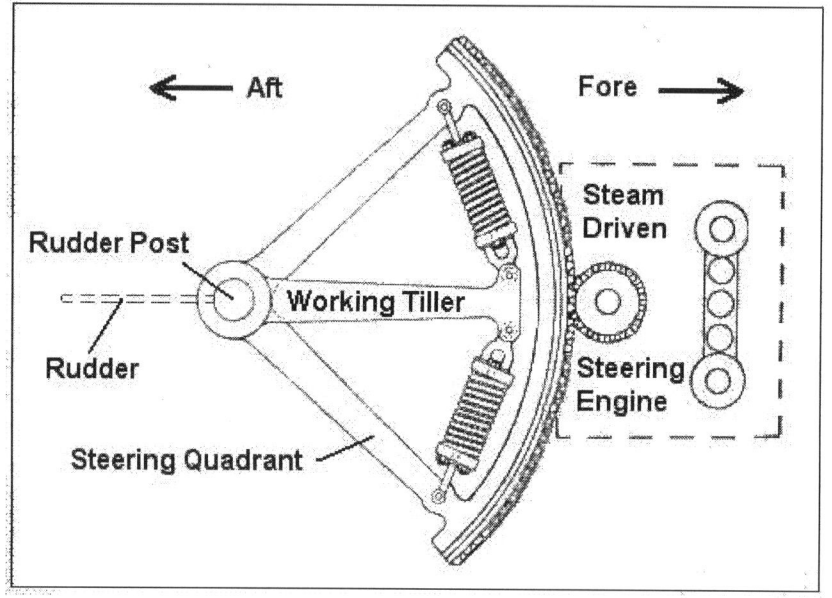

Fig. P-06 Wilson and Pirrie's elastic steering quadrant.

Tonnage, Volume and Displacement

Next we come to the topic of ship tonnage which was usually expressed in gross registered tons and net registered tons.

Gross registered tonnage (GRT) represented the total internal volume of a vessel, not its weight. One register ton is equal to a volume of 100 cubic feet. RMS *Olympic* was listed as a 45,324 GRT vessel. Her total internal volume was 4,532,400 cubic feet.

Net registered tonnage (NRT) represented the internal volume of the ship that was available for passengers and cargo expressed in register tons, where one register ton is equal to a volume of 100 cubic feet. NRT is obtained by subtracting the volume of non revenue earning spaces (i.e., spaces not available for carrying passengers or cargo) from the ship's GRT. In 1911, RMS *Olympic* had an NRT of 20,894 tons.

A ship's weight is specified by her displacement, which equals the weight in long tons of the volume of water that is displaced (i.e., pushed aside) by the vessel's underwater volume when afloat. The weight of the displaced water equals the total weight of the vessel. RMS *Olympic* displaced about 52,000 long tons of sea water. HMS *Hawke* displaced about 7,700 long tons of sea water. One long ton of sea water occupies a volume of about 35 cubic feet and weighs 2,240 pounds (lbs).

Lengths, Distances and Depth

Distances were expressed in nautical miles (usually referred to simply as miles), cables, or yards, depending how far away an object was from the observer. One nautical mile is 6,080 feet. One cable is 608 feet, or exactly 1/10 of a nautical mile. Since there are 3 feet in a yard, one cable is a little over 200 yards.

Depth was usually express in fathoms or feet. One fathom is equal to 6 feet. The depth of water that was marked on a chart was usually given in fathoms for some average state of tide, such as mean low tide. These length relationships are shown in Figure P-07 below.

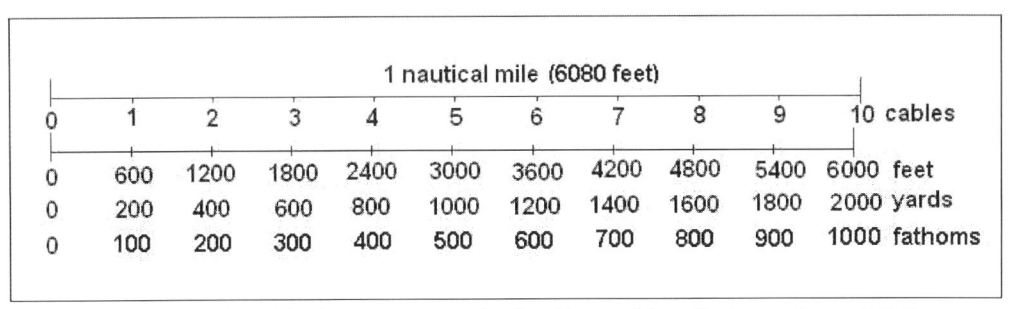

1 nautical mile (6080 feet)										
0	1	2	3	4	5	6	7	8	9	10 cables
0	600	1200	1800	2400	3000	3600	4200	4800	5400	6000 feet
0	200	400	600	800	1000	1200	1400	1600	1800	2000 yards
0	100	200	300	400	500	600	700	800	900	1000 fathoms

Fig. P-07 **Relationship between nautical miles, cables, feet, yards and fathoms.**

Speed and Knots

Finally there is the concept of speed. The speed of a vessel was, and still is, expressed in terms of knots, with 1 knot equal to 1 nautical mile per hour. For a steamship, the average speed through the water was approximately proportional to the average number of revolutions per minute (rpm) carried on her engines, which in turn, were usually connected directly to the ship's propellers by means of shafts and thrust collars. The conversion from revolutions per minute to speed in knots was a function of the pitch of the propellers (the ideal travel distance that the propellers would move in one revolution if there were no slippage through the water) and the amount of slip produced by the propellers at a given rotational speed (the difference between the ideal travel distance and the actual travel distance in one revolution of the propellers). The amount of slip depended on a number of things, including the resistance of the ship's hull, which itself was a function of how clean the ship's bottom was.

A table, called a slip table, showing the expected speed of the vessel as a function of revolutions per minute would be posted in the chartroom once that was worked out by measuring how long it took for the ship to advanced some known distance (for example a measured mile or other known distance) while carrying a given number of revolutions.

Propeller Revolutions (RPM)	Knots by Propeller	Speed of Ship (Knots)	Percent Slip
50	17.02	15.48	9.0%
55	18.73	16.79	10.4%
60	20.43	18.07	11.5%
65	22.13	19.34	12.6%
70	23.83	20.59	13.6%
75	25.53	21.83	14.5%
80	27.24	23.06	15.3%
85	28.94	24.27	16.1%

Fig. P-08 Example of a derived slip table for an *Olympic* class vessel.

Another measure of a ship's speed through the water was by means of the patent log. The patent log ideally measured the distance traveled through the water over some specified time interval. On White Star Line passenger vessels, the log was usually reset at noon every day, and readings were taken by the ship's quartermasters every two hours. The patent log used on *Olympic* was a Walker's Patent Neptune Taffrail Log which was mounted on the rail of the docking bridge near the stern of the vessel.

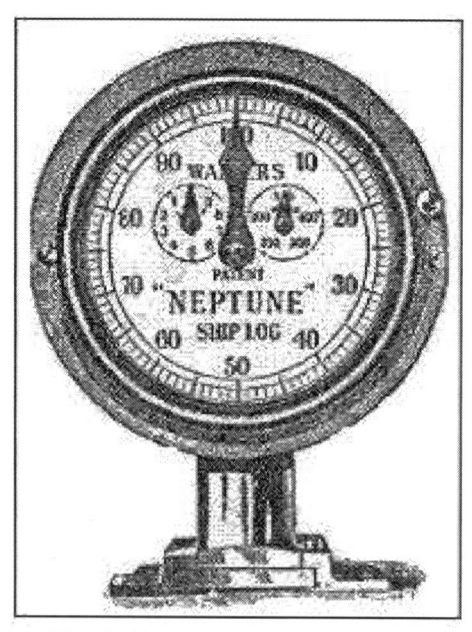

Fig. P-09 A Neptune patent log.

The small dial on the left rotated once every nautical mile and was marked in tenths of a mile. The large dial in the middle rotated once every 100 nautical miles and had 100 units marked around the dial. The small dial on the right rotated once every 500 nautical miles and was marked in 100 mile increments.

Although calibrated in nautical miles, what the taffrail log actually measured was the number of revolutions of a finned rotor that was attached to the end of a long line as it was pulled through the water by the moving vessel. Its accuracy in recording nautical miles depended on how well it was calibrated at different speeds, when it was calibrated last, and its overall condition, including the attached log line and all internal parts.

It must be emphasized, that speed through the water was not necessarily the same as the actual speed-made-good of the vessel. For example, if a vessel was traveling at 15 knots through the water against a 1 knot head current, its speed-made-good would actually be 14 knots, something that would be noted by comparing the actual distance traveled relative to known landmarks or navigational fixes over a given period of time.

Today, the term "knots" has only one exclusive meaning, and that is nautical miles per hour, a measure of speed. Unfortunately, many seafarers back in 1911 erroneously used the term "knots" when referring to distance in nautical miles. Even in printed engine log books as late as the 1930's you may see a column marked "Knots Run" to mean nautical miles traveled by the ship over a specified interval of time, or another column marked "Knots by Propeller" where someone would record the distance traveled in nautical miles based on the propeller's pitch and the total number of propeller revolutions that were counted over a specified interval of time. Sometimes you may also hear sailors use the erroneous term "knots per hour" when referring to speed. Despite some of these misuses of the term "knots" by some seafarers, their true meaning can easily be obtained from the context of what they were saying.

PROLOGUE

Samuel Halpern

In 1869 the steamer *Narragansett* was overtaken by the steamer *Providence* going northward up the East River in New York. The slower *Narragansett* then found herself being "towed" magically upriver by the faster *Providence* without having to make any changes to steam or engines. When the vessels got into the Hell Gate, a treacherous tidal strait in the East River, the equilibrium became too unstable, and slower *Narragansett* plunged into the quarter of the faster *Providence*.

In 1871 a collision was reported between the steam tug *General William McCandless* and the steam tug *Unit* when the faster *McCandless*, which was passing *Unit* on her starboard side, suddenly dropped astern and veered into the starboard quarter of *Unit* causing *Unit* to swerve around to starboard and throw her stem against the port side of a the ferryboat *Commodore Perry* which was passing both tugs to starboard.

In 1878 the tug *Hartt* was being overtaken by the excursion steamer *City of Brockton*. When the bow of *Brockton* was about 100 feet ahead on the starboard hand of *Hartt*, the tug suddenly took a sheer toward *Brockton* and struck her in the port quarter.

In 1885 there was a collision between the Cunard Liner *Aurania* and the White Star Liner *Republic* in Gebney's Channel near the fairway buoys as both were leaving New York harbor. *Republic* had her stem broken off while *Aurania* had her port counter damaged. Again, the overtaken vessel veered under the quarter of the passing vessel.

Fifteen years later a similar collision took place under similar circumstances in almost the same exact place between the steamers *Martello* and *Mesaba* on 22 September 1900. In this case *Mesaba* was making about 13 knots and *Martello* about 10 knots and somewhat ahead of *Mesaba*. After giving a passing signal of two whistles indicating that she was going to port, *Mesaba* put her engines at full ahead passing the slower *Martello* to the north in the channel. When *Martello*'s stem was abeam *Mesaba*'s amidships or a little aft, *Martello*'s bow was seen to veer to port toward *Mesaba* until she struck about 100 feet forward of *Mesaba*'s stern.

Despite a number of other similar cases, the fundamental cause of collisions such as these was not well understood and was considered a mystery for many years. Even in 1911, and despite a growing number of so called "suction theories" being advanced in some nautical circles, most practical mariners did not believe that forces of attraction or repulsion could take place as a result of ships steaming past each other in restricted waterways, or that the shallowness of the bottom could have an effect on the vessels involved.

On the 20th of September 1911 the White Star Liner RMS *Olympic*, coming out of Southampton Water, was making a turn to port around the West Bramble buoy in the Solent north of the Isle of Wight. At the same time, HMS *Hawke*, a protected cruiser of the Royal Navy, was making a turn to starboard around Egypt Point, a prominent landmark on the north side of the Isle of Wight to the south. As the two vessels completed their respective turns they steadied on what appeared to be almost parallel courses in the channel with *Olympic* accelerating rapidly towards her full ahead speed for restricted waters. As *Olympic* drew ahead of *Hawke*, the much smaller cruiser unexpectedly veered sharply to port, as if her helm was starboarded, and struck the massive White Star Liner in her starboard quarter. As a result of the collision, both vessels suffered severe damage and had to return to port for repairs.

The following was written about the cause of the accident in an article that appeared the next day in *The New York Times*:

Collision Unexplained.

How the collision occurred is a mystery. Everybody agrees that the two ships were steaming parallel with one another, neither at high speed, and that suddenly, unaccountably, and amazingly, the *Hawke* swung around and crashed into the *Olympic*'s starboard side near the stern.

What really happened that September day in 1911 in the Solent? Was it merely a case of innocent suction that caused the accident, or a case of negligent navigation on part of one or both vessels?

Chapter I

"THERE'S GOING TO BE A COLLISION"

Samuel Halpern

It was 11:10am on Wednesday, 20 September 1911, when the 52,000 ton displacement White Star Liner *Olympic* departed Southampton carrying more than 1,300 passengers. Her next stop was to be Cherbourg, France to pick up additional passengers and mails, and then onto Queenstown, Ireland for more passengers and mails before crossing the Atlantic to New York. Over 2,100 passengers were expected to be taken on board for this, the outbound leg of her fifth round trip voyage to New York. She was to follow the same route she took about three weeks earlier when she crossed the Atlantic traveling a total distance of 2,781 nautical miles at an average speed of 21.81 knots in 5 days, 7 hours and 29 minutes,[1] her second best westbound crossing speed since her maiden voyage back on 14 June 1911.[2]

On the bridge in overall command of *Olympic* that fine September day was Captain Edward J. Smith, the same man who had commanded *Olympic* on all four of her previous voyages. He was also the man who would later command *Olympic*'s ill fated sister ship *Titanic* on her maiden voyage in April 1912. To guide *Olympic* on her journey down Southampton Water into the Solent and then out to the Nab Light Vessel located off the east coast of the Isle of Wight was Trinity House harbour pilot George Bowyer, having handled *Olympic* in these same confined waters on all four previous voyages. Also on the bridge was *Olympic*'s fourth officer David Alexander who was working the engine order telegraphs, and *Olympic*'s sixth officer Harold Holehouse who was responsible for recording events and taking the time off the wheelhouse clock for the ship's scrap log. At the wheel in the center of the navigating bridge, just forward of the enclosed wheelhouse, was Quartermaster (QM) Albert Haines.

Fig. 1-01 *Olympic*'s **navigating bridge.**

Stationed forward on the forecastle head for the trip down Southampton Water was Chief Officer Henry Tingle Wilde. Stationed aft on the poop was First Officer William McMaster Murdoch. In the crow's nest, along with two lookout men, was Second Officer Robert Hume. And stationed on the standard compass platform amidships, also referred to as the ship's conning tower, was Fifth Officer Adolphus Tulloch.

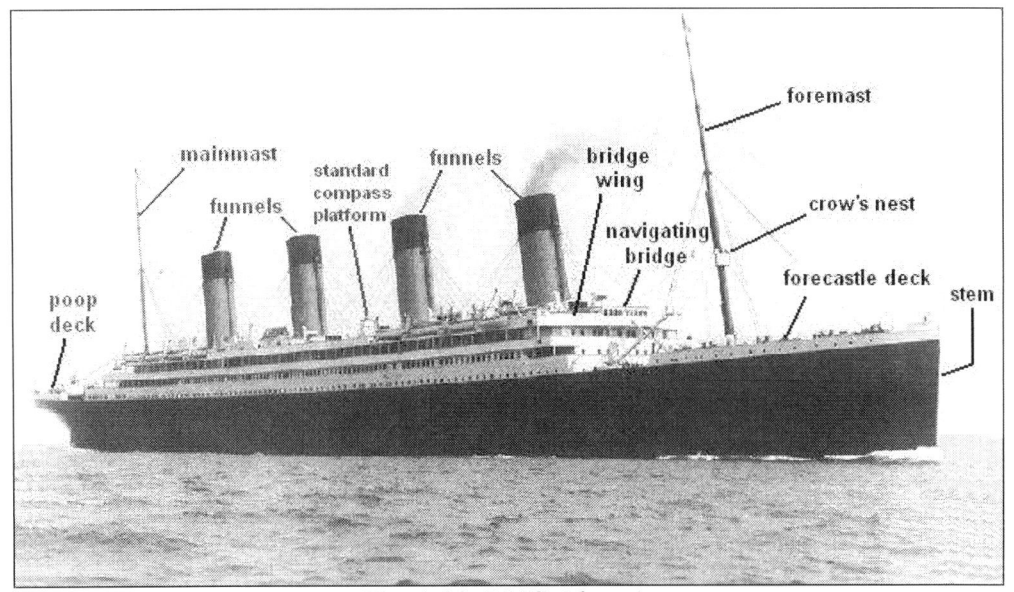

Fig. 1-02 RMS *Olympic*.

At about the same time *Olympic* departed Southampton's Ocean Dock, HMS *Hawke*, a first class protected cruiser of 7,700 tons displacement, had just passed the Nab End buoy east of the Isle of Wight heading northwestward toward Spithead. All that morning *Hawke* was engage in a full power trial under natural draught conditions carrying an average of 92 revolutions per minute on her engines, and averaging about 17 knots. At 11:30am *Hawke*'s full power trial ended and a 3/5 power trial under natural draught began. The course for that 3/5 power trial would take her from Spithead, up the Solent, past Cowes, down the Western Solent toward the Needles Channel. Her intention was to go down as far as the Solent Bank, turn around, and then to go back up and head back out to the Nab. Under 3/5 power, her engines were producing 82 revolutions per minute, and her speed was a little over 15 knots.

In charge of *Hawke* was Commander William F. Blunt. Attending to recording the times and maneuvers for the power trials was *Hawke*'s navigation officer Lt. Reginald Aylen. The officer of the watch (OOW) until noon was Lt. McGregor Robertson.

At noontime the air temperature was 64°F, the barometer measured 29.55 inches, and the wind was out of the WSW displaying moderate to strong breezes. Skies were described as overcast with some detached clouds. There were also some passing, squally showers.

About 12:20pm, 50 minutes after her 3/5 power trial began, *Hawke* had the Solent Bank buoy abeam and turned around to go back up the West Solent. Her course by standard compass was N77E [061° T], the reciprocal of the course she took heading down the West Solent but transposed about 900 feet closer to the Isle of Wight which was now on her starboard hand as she headed back up. About five minutes after turning the buoy, Commander Blunt went down to lunch leaving Lt. Aylen in charge of the bridge. The time on *Hawke*'s deck clock was about 12:25pm.

Fig. 1-03 HMS *Hawke*.

At 12:27pm,[3] as she was coming down Southampton Water, *Olympic*'s engines were put at half-ahead. Two minutes later, at 12:29pm, *Olympic* had Calshot Castle off her starboard beam, and a minute later, at 12:30pm, her central turbine engine was disconnected as her reciprocating engines were ordered to slow-ahead as she passed the Blackjack buoy to take the sharp turn around the Calshot Spit into the Thorn Channel.[4] (See area chart in Figure 1-05.) It was the start of a complex reverse "S" maneuver that would eventually take her into the East Solent just south of the Ryde Middle, a shoal bank formed of mud, shells, gravel, and sand that divides the east branch of the Solent into two navigable channels. From the channel south of the Ryde Middle, *Olympic* would head out for the Nab light vessel off the east coast of the Isle of Wight where the pilot was to be dropped off before crossing the English Channel to Cherbourg.

About the same time that *Olympic* was passing the Blackjack buoy, *Hawke*'s quartermaster, Petty Officer 1st Class (PO1) Ernest Hunt, came up on deck to relieve the quartermaster who was then conning the vessel. The course to steer given to him was already marked on the blackboard. It read N77½E. Shortly after, Leading Seaman Henry Yeates came up to relieve the helmsman at the wheel, and he too was given the course to steer. Keeping lookout high up on *Hawke*'s foremast at the time was Able Bodied (AB) Seaman Alfred Crookham.

At 12:34pm, by her wheelhouse clock, *Olympic* had the Calshot Spit buoy abeam as she was being steadied on a course of S65W magnetic [229° T] to take the Thorn Channel. Within a minute, at 12:35pm, her turbine engine was connected back up after her engine-order telegraphs were again put to full-ahead by order of the pilot.

About the same time on *Hawke*, Lt. Geoffery Bashford came up from lunch to take over as officer of the watch. As he arrived on deck he noticed *Olympic* coming down the Thorn Channel bearing about 3 points on his port bow several miles distant with her port side just opening up to him.

About two minutes later, 12:37pm by *Olympic*'s wheelhouse clock, *Olympic* passed the North Thorn buoy while accelerating on all three engines toward her full-ahead channel speed for restricted waters of about 20 knots.[5] It was about then that *Hawke* was sighted 3 to 3 ½ miles distant and about ½ to 1 point off *Olympic*'s port bow by Captain Smith and pilot George Bowyer. At the time, *Hawke* had just passed the Gurnard Ledge buoy on her starboard hand.

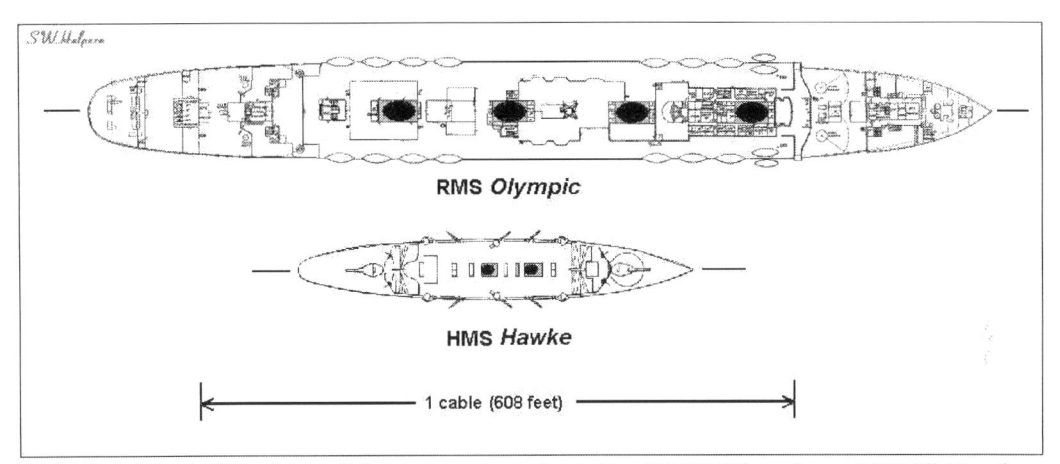

Fig. 1-04 Relative sizes of the two vessels involve; RMS *Olympic* and HMS *Hawke*.

At 12:40pm *Olympic* came abeam the Thorn Knoll buoy and Bowyer gave the order to helmsman Haines to "starboard easy" and telegraphed the engine room to put the port engine slow-ahead to take the channel down to the West Bramble buoy.[6] The central turbine engine was then disconnected as the ship started an easy turn to port. It was about this time on *Hawke* that Commander Blunt came back up from below and went to the standard compass on top of *Hawke*'s bridge where Lt. Aylen and Lt. Bashford were waiting. Stationed on the bridge below were QM Hunt, AB Yeates, and signalman Albert Porter. Coming up ahead on their starboard side was Egypt Point, a prominent landmark and small lighthouse located on the northern end of West Cowes on the Isle of Wight. It was Blunt's intention to take an easy turn to starboard when abreast Egypt Point to put *Hawke* on a course of S85E magnetic [079° T]. This course would take her into the East Solent north of the Ryde Middle. Bearing about 4 points off his port bow, between the Thorn Knoll and West Bramble buoys, was *Olympic*. Soon two puffs of steam were seen coming from *Olympic*'s whistle when she was about 2/3 the distance down from Thorn Knoll to West Bramble indicating that she was going to take the turn to port to round the West Bramble buoy into the East Solent. It was then that Commander Blunt decided to alter his course to S74E magnetic [090° T] to give *Olympic* as much room as possible after remarking to Lt. Aylen that *Olympic* was going to take the eastern channel. Egypt Point was then coming up about 1 point before *Hawke*'s starboard beam.

At 12:42pm by her wheelhouse clock, *Olympic* was abreast the West Bramble buoy and Bowyer ordered QM Haines to put the helm "hard-astarboard" (left full rudder) to take the turn around the buoy. He then ordered the port engine to "stop," followed soon after to "half-astern," and finally to "full-astern" to help sharpen the turn around the buoy.

Meanwhile, just moments before on *Hawke*, Blunt ordered "15 port" to helmsman Yeates who gave *Hawke* 15° of right rudder. According to Blunt, *Hawke* was then about 3 ½ cables [700 yards] abreast of Egypt Point. When *Hawke* came round to S74E on her standard compass, Blunt gave the order to "steady." On the steering compass, the course showed S75E.[7] Soon after, Blunt ordered his helmsman to "Steady on the *Edgar*," a cruiser of the same class as *Hawke* that was anchored in Stokes Bay that could be seen several miles away almost directly ahead of them.

Meanwhile, as *Olympic* was completing her turn around the West Bramble buoy, Bowyer ordered Haines to "ease the helm" which allowed the helm to swing back to amidships. Then came the order to "steady up" and Haines turned his wheel a few spokes to his right to stop *Olympic*'s swing and bring her up onto a course of S64E as seen on the steering compass in front of him. As *Olympic* steadied following the turn, her fifth officer, Adolphus Tulloch, rang three bells on the push bell on the standard compass platform signaling the bridge that he had *Olympic* on the prearranged compass course to take her south of the Ryde Middle, a course that *Olympic* would have maintained until abreast the Peel Bank buoy which lay a few miles ahead. On the standard compass in front of Tulloch the lubber line read S59E.[8] It was about then that Bowyer ordered *Olympic*'s port engine, which had been running full-astern, be put to stop and then to full-speed ahead. Down in *Olympic*'s engine room the reversing gear for the port engine was put over from astern to ahead, and the turbine engine was put back on line with the throw of a lever. The time noted was 12:44pm. Now with all three engines running up to full-ahead, *Olympic* began to accelerate once again toward her full-ahead speed under reduced steam of about 20 knots for restricted waters. According to Bowyer, *Olympic* was about 2 to 3 ship lengths south of the West Bramble buoy when she was steadied onto her new courseline.

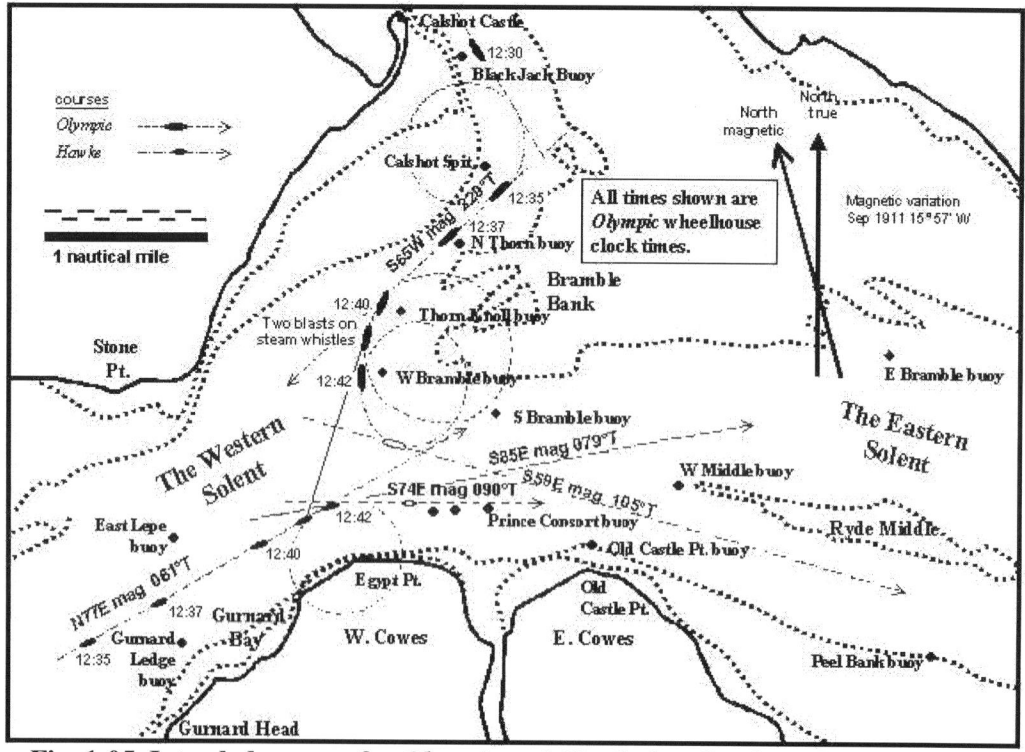

Fig. 1-05 Intended courses for *Olympic* and *Hawke* heading into the East Solent.

The diagram in Figure 1-05 shows the approximate situation for both vessels up to about 12:42pm, *Olympic* time, when *Olympic* was abreast the West Bramble buoy taking the turn into the east Solent.

Up to and including the time that *Olympic* signaled *Hawke* that she was going to take the turn around the West Bramble buoy, the courses and positions for each vessel for the times shown on the chart in Figure 1-05 more or less agree with what witnesses for both sides claimed in evidence before the High Court of Justice in the trial that followed in November 1911. However, their stories as to what happened as each ship completed her turn and afterward tend to differ greatly.

According to those on *Olympic*, after *Olympic* steadied on her course of S59E magnetic, *Hawke* was seen about 2 to 3 points off her starboard quarter about ¼ nautical mile back heading on a course that appeared to be pointing a little to the north of the course that *Olympic* was on. Soon after, *Hawke* was seen to be running on a course that appeared to be parallel to, and about 1 ½ cables [300 yards] apart from that of *Olympic*. As *Olympic* had slowed to about 11 or 12 knots coming out of the turn around the buoy, *Hawke* became the overtaking vessel, coming up from more than two points abaft *Olympic*'s starboard beam. *Hawke* continued to gain on *Olympic* until she came up as far as *Olympic*'s bridge before starting to drop back as *Olympic*'s speed kept increasing with all engines running full-ahead. Then, unexpectedly, as *Hawke*'s stem dropped back to about *Olympic*'s amidships point, Captain Smith called out to George Bowyer, "He is starboarding and he is going to hit us."

According to those on *Hawke*, *Olympic* was still making her turn around the West Bramble buoy when *Hawke* steadied onto a course of S74E magnetic. When *Olympic* finally appeared to complete her turn, her bow was in line with *Hawke*'s stern at a distance between 1 and 1 ½ cables away [200 to 300 yards]. *Olympic*'s heading appeared to be a little to the south of the courseline that *Hawke* was on. As *Hawke* approached the middle of three buoys near the entrance to Cowes on the Isle of Wight, a red and white chequered buoy, Commander Blunt remarked to his navigation officer Lt. Aylen that "*Olympic* was unpleasantly close." The two ships now appeared to be on nearly parallel courses about ½ cable [100 yards] apart with *Olympic*'s bow in-line with *Hawke*'s bridge and quickly drawing ahead. When *Hawke* came up to the Prince Consort buoy, the easternmost of the three buoys near the entrance to Cowes, Blunt called for 5° of port helm (right rudder) to turn his ship to starboard and for his helmsman to steady on the No Man's Land Fort which could be seen about 15 degrees off their starboard bow about 8 miles away.

Fig. 1-06 No Man's Land Fort.

Soon after the order to steady on the "right hand fort" was given, Lt. Bashford, the OOW, ordered QM Hunt to take over the wheel from seaman Yeates, as he was not too happy with how well Yeates was handling the wheel as *Olympic* was passing about 100 yards away and increasing speed rapidly. Before Hunt was able to get *Hawke* steadied onto the fort, *Hawke* unexpectedly stopped turning to starboard and began to swing back to port. It was then that Blunt called down, "What are you doing? Port, Port, Hard-aport!" as *Hawke* took an exceptional swerve toward *Olympic*. Within about a minute, and despite reversing his engines to full astern, *Hawke* struck *Olympic* about 90 feet ahead of her stern while carrying 15° of right rudder with a jammed helm.

On *Olympic*, the entries put down in the ship's scrap log by Sixth Officer Harold Holehouse were:

12.46 Struck on starboard quarter by HM's ship.
 Warning bell rung, watertight doors closed from bridge.
12.47 Stop as required.

The only thing that both sides seemed to agree upon was that the two vessels were on what appeared to be converging courses of about 15 degrees after each ship came out of their respective turns; *Hawke* around Egypt Point and *Olympic* around the West Bramble buoy. As can be seen from the chart in Figure 1-05, this much checks out if *Olympic* steadied on S59E magnetic as claimed, and *Hawke* steadied on S74E magnetic as claimed. But the positions of both vessels relative to each other is nowhere near to what each side claimed if *Olympic* steadied at the position shown (about 3 ship lengths south of the West Bramble buoy) and *Hawke* steadied on a line taking her close to the line of buoys near the entrance to Cowes. The only other point of agreement was that the two vessels later appeared to be on almost parallel courses for some short amount of time before *Hawke* started an inexplicable turn toward *Olympic*.

We will examine what each side claimed in much greater detail in subsequent chapters. However, it is interesting to first see how the collision took shape according to a few independent sources, and a few not so independent sources.

One independent eyewitness account was published in *The New York Times* the day after the collision. It came from a Cowes boatman, Ruben Speed, and is reproduced below in Figure 1-07:

> Reuben Speed, a Cowes boatman, who happened to be close by at the moment of the collision, gave the following account of it:
>
> I was with a photographer, who had just taken a picture of the liner. She had come out of Southampton Water and rounded the West Bramble buoy, and was proceeding eastward when we saw the Hawke coming up from the west. She had been down for some trials, and was steaming pretty fast, but slowed a little as she came up with the Olympic.
>
> "They steamed alongside of one another for some little way, then all of a sudden the Hawke turned in. I said to my companion, 'there's going to be a collision. Look, she'll hit her.' He said, 'No, the Hawke will go under her stern.'
>
> "Just at that moment the Hawke hit the Olympic a tremendous blow—so it looked to us—on the starboard side, some seventy-eight feet from her stern.
>
> "When the Hawke began to turn she was about abreast of the Olympic's foremost funnel, so you can see that very little time passed before she struck her. It was then 12:50 and the weather was clear except for a slight drizzling rain.

Fig. 1-07 Account of Reuben Speed from *The New York Times*, 21 September 1911.

Another independent eyewitness, Lt. W. C. Nixon of the United States Navy, was a passenger on board *Olympic* when the accident happened. Nixon had this to say in an article that he wrote for the US *Naval Institute Proceedings* (Vol. 37, 1911) that was published later that year:

> "I came up on the starboard side of the promenade deck of the *Olympic* at the instant she blew two blasts on her whistle...*Hawke* [was] coming up the channel from the Solent, about the same distance from the intersection [of the channels] as the *Olympic*, and rather more than that from the *Olympic* herself...*Olympic* was making at least 15 knots and probably her speed was nearer 18 knots...and as far as I could learn held her speed. I am not certain whether the *Hawke* paid any attention or made any acknowledgment to these blasts, and apparently she too was holding her speed. As both vessels approached the main channel, it was evident that the *Olympic* would turn first by a slight margin...While yet a quarter of a mile away, however, the *Hawke* slowed (I estimate this from the disappearance of her bow wave) and fell in line behind the *Olympic*...Believing that the danger of collision was gone, I passed on around the bow to the port side of the *Olympic*. Perhaps three to five minutes later I crossed again to the starboard side...The *Olympic* had just completed her turn and had straightened on her new course. The *Hawke* was coming up fast, on a parallel course, perhaps 100 to 200 yards from the *Olympic*, and just beginning to 'lap' her...A few seconds afterward the *Hawke* swung almost instantly, pivoting apparently on her center, and seemed to leap out of the water toward the *Olympic*. She struck the *Olympic* almost exactly at right angles at a point about 75 feet forward of *Olympic*'s stern."

Col. Sexton White was a first class passenger on board *Olympic* traveling with his daughter to America. He was a member of the Institute of Civil Engineers and the Institute of Naval Architects, and testified on behalf of *Olympic* at the High Court trial in November. He said he first saw *Hawke* at a distance of 3 to 4 miles when *Olympic* was passing the Calshot Spit buoy going down the Thorn Channel. He crossed over to the starboard side of the promenade deck when he heard *Olympic* sound two blasts on her whistles, and was watching *Hawke* the entire time after he crossed over. When he first reached the starboard side of the deck, *Olympic* was approaching *Hawke*. After *Olympic* completed her turn around the West Bramble buoy, *Hawke* was 400 to 500 yards off *Olympic*'s starboard quarter. At that time, according to him, *Hawke* was distinctly the faster of the two vessels and was gaining on *Olympic* until her stem came a bit forward of where he was standing, which was near the first class entrance on the Promenade deck, before she started to drop back. The distance that the two ships were apart seemed to be about 300 yards, and they appeared to be running on parallel courses. Then, when *Hawke*'s stem was about amidships of *Olympic*, it looked to him that *Hawke* had starboarded her helm (turning her bow to port) with the intent to cross under *Olympic*'s stern. "I thought she was making a very narrow shave of it." *Hawke* then struck *Olympic* at what appeared to be a right angle. Following the collision, *Hawke* recovered from a heavy roll and her bow gradually twisted forward to the same direction that *Olympic* was facing having been pulled forward by the massive passenger liner.

Henry Lashmar, master of the steam yacht *Bellinda*, also testified on behalf of the White Star Line at the High Court trial in November. Lashmar said that he was standing in the bows of his yacht when he saw *Olympic* come down Southampton Water. His yacht was moored about ¼ mile S by W of the Prince Consort buoy in Cowes Roads facing eastward against the westward setting ebb tide. At the time *Olympic* sounded two blasts on her whistles as she approached the West Bramble buoy, Lashmar's attention turned to *Hawke*. As she was coming up the Solent, *Hawke* appeared to eclipse the East Lepe buoy which could be seen well away to the west. Lashmar estimated that *Hawke* was about mid way between the buoy and the shoreline of the Isle of Wight. He saw *Hawke* make the turn around Egypt Point toward the east, and said he thought she was only about 300 yards [1 ½ cables] from the shore as she was coming around. After seeing *Olympic* complete her turn around the Bramble, *Hawke* appeared to be about 3 of her lengths (about 2 cables) behind *Olympic* on a course that at first appeared to be slightly converging with that of *Olympic*. He also thought that *Hawke* was going about 4 knots faster than the White Star Liner, and estimated that *Hawke* was making about 16 knots based on the appearance of her bow wave. He then said that *Hawke* overhauled *Olympic* after coming onto a course that appeared to be parallel with that of *Olympic*, and as the two vessels came abreast the Prince Consort buoy, "*Hawke* suddenly turned into *Olympic*." He placed the point of the collision about ¼ mile NNE of the buoy.

Fig. 1-08 *Hawke* **(far left) and** *Olympic* **(far right) just minutes after the collision.**

Also testifying for the White Star Line was Albert Frederick Masters, Chief Fishery officer for the southwest district, and former commander of tramp steamers and holder of a pilot's license for districts on the south coast. About 20 minutes to one, Masters left a meeting of the Committee of the Fisheries Board at Town Hall to go down to the Esplanade by the Royal Yacht Squadron (located on the northeast coast of West Cowes) for the expressed purpose of seeing *Olympic* pass by. When he got there, he was rewarded when the mighty White Star Line passenger steamer came into his view from round the club house with the landing stage of the Squadron on his port hand and the Victoria Pier directly behind him. "She was out in the alignment, north from where I was standing. The West Bramble buoy was just in sight." Then *Hawke* came into view, "I saw the *Hawke*, she blotted out part of the *Olympic* from me…Part of the quarter – part of the starboard side [of *Olympic*]…About one-third of her…" Masters was not able to judge how far *Hawke* was from *Olympic* when she shut in her quarter, but soon *Hawke* was abeam and "about half a mile" away from where he was standing. He then watched for "just a minute or so" and then saw *Hawke* turn to port and collide into *Olympic*.

George Lee was the Superintendent of the Trinity House Southeast District on Trinity Warf on East Cowes. He along with district clerk and storekeeper John Gaudion were watching *Olympic* come "passing through the [Cowes] Roads and a cruiser coming past her" from the store on the upper floor of the south side of Trinity House. When Lee first saw the two ships there was a space of daylight between *Hawke*'s stem and *Olympic*'s stern. There appeared to be a very perceptible difference in speed between the two vessels as *Hawke* appeared to be overtaking.

Lee said that he noticed *Hawke* come up to where her stem seemed to be in line with *Olympic*'s third funnel as seen from where he and Gaudion were standing. Then *Olympic* started to draw ahead, and *Hawke* then appeared to have starboarded her helm with the intent of going under *Olympic*'s stern. From where they both were standing, they did not witness the collision itself as part of the roof of the building partially blocked their view. Both, George Lee and John Gaudion, testified on behalf of the White Star Line at the High Court of Justice trial.

The chart below (Figure 1-09) shows the locations of Henry Lashmar who was on his steam yacht *Bellinda*, Albert Masters who was on the promenade by the Royal Yacht Squadron on West Cowes, and George Lee and John Gaudion who were on the upper floor of Trinity House on East Cowes.

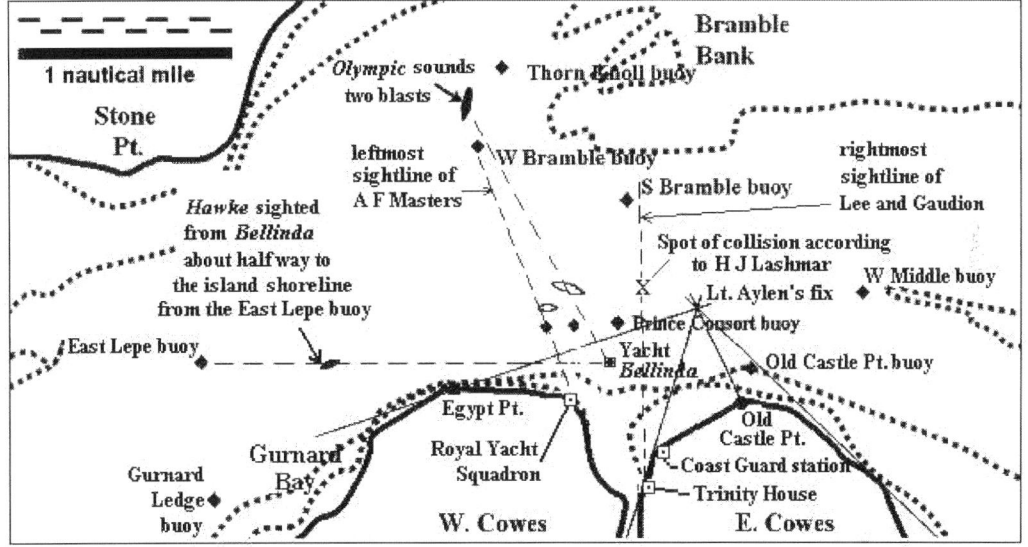

Fig. 1-09 Locations of WSL witnesses: Henry Lashmar (yacht *Billinda*), Albert Masters (Royal Yacht Squadron), George Lee and John Gaudion (Trinity House).

---

[1] The crossing across the Atlantic began with departure taken at 3:11pm GMT on 31 August 1911 off the Daunt's Rock light vessel outside Queenstown harbor to her arrival at 5:40pm New York mean time on 5 September 1911 off the Ambrose Channel light vessel outside of New York harbor.

[2] On her third westbound crossing, *Olympic* averaged 21.83 knots over the slightly longer southern route.

[3] *Olympic*'s wheelhouse clock was running about a minute ahead of *Hawke*'s deck clock.

[4] *Olympic* was a triple screw steamer with two reciprocating engines, each turning a large three-bladed wing propeller, and a single turbine engine turning a four-bladed central propeller. The turbine engine was fed from exhaust steam coming from the reciprocating engines, and produced about 1/3 of *Olympic*'s total thrust horsepower. For speeds less than one-half, or when going astern, the turbine engine was disengaged, and exhaust steam from the reciprocating engines was redirected to the ship's two main condensers.

[5] This information came from Captain Smith on day 1 of the trail before the High Court. Under reduced steam coming in and out of port, Smith said that full speed was about 20 knots carrying about 75 revolutions per minute (rpm), half speed was 15 knots carrying 50 rpm, and slow speed was 8 to 9 knots carrying 30 rpm. The central turbine engine was shut off unless going full or half ahead, and Smith agreed that full ahead speed for the ocean was about 22 ½ knots. The exact same information was given by Chief Engineer Robert Fleming on day 2 of the trial. Information from *Olympic* engineer Charles McKimm following a collision with the Furness Bermuda liner *Fort St. George* in 1924 was that in closed waters full ahead was restricted to 65 rpm, half ahead to 55 rpm, slow ahead to 35 rpm, and dead slow ahead to about 20 to 25 rpm. A study of *Olympic* performance showed that *Olympic* would obtain a speed of almost 19 ½ knots carrying 65 rpm, and would obtain 20 knots carrying 68 rpm. (See article by S. W. Halpern, "Speed and Revolutions," available on-line at:
http://www.titanicology.com/Titanica/SpeedAndRevolutions.htm.)

[6] In 1911 the order to "starboard the helm" meant to turn the wheel to the left which put the tiller over to the right (to starboard) thereby moving the rudder, which pointed aft, to the left. When it was said that a ship "starboarded" it meant that her *stern* swung out to starboard (to the right) as her head turned to port (to the left). This terminology was standard at the time, and came down from the days of sail. The order to "port the helm" meant just the opposite.

[7] In general, the steering compass and standard compass differed by a few degrees from each other due to differences in compass deviation error caused by the distribution of steel and iron in a vessel. Because of its placement, a ship's standard compass generally had less deviation error. It should also be noted that magnetic north is not the same as true north. The difference is a function of location, which for the Solent in September of 1911, was 15° 57' W. This difference is referred to as magnetic variation.

[8] The difference between *Olympic*'s standard compass and the steering compass on that particular heading was 5 degrees due to differences in compass deviation error.

Chapter II

A ONE-SIDED ENQUIRY

Mark Chirnside

On the same day that the collision had taken place, *Hawke*'s commander, officers and other crewmen wrote witness statements about what had happened while the incident was fresh in their minds. The following day, 21 September 1911, Admiral Moore, the Commander-in-Chief at Portsmouth, directed two naval captains, Captain Henry W. Grant of HMS *Dryad* and Captain Edward L. Booty of HMS *Ariadne*, to investigate the circumstances of the collision. Wasting no time, he instructed them to assemble on board the damaged *Hawke* on the morning of 22 September 1911 and to "hold a strict and careful enquiry" guided by Chapter XVIII of the King's Regulations. The naval authorities wanted to investigate what had caused the collision between the largest steamer in the world and one of the Royal Navy's enormous fleet in one of the busiest shipping channels.

Although "strict and careful," the enquiry was hardly a comprehensive one when compared to the numerous legal proceedings that followed it. Altogether, all of the witnesses were asked 187 questions, based on the statements that they had already completed. Commander Blunt himself answered almost one third of them.

Engineer Commander G. E. A. Crichton's account was a single paragraph that occupied most of a foolscap piece of paper. He described the working of the engines "at 82 revs: which they had been doing steadily since noon to carry out the steam trial." At 12:48pm, he described the telegraph being "altered from half speed ahead to stop, immediately followed by full speed astern. The stop valve was partly closed and the reversing gear run over, the main engines going from ahead to astern without stopping." He felt the "lurch" of the collision, which was followed by an order to close the watertight doors, and the engines were stopped two minutes later.

Signalman Albert Edward Porter wrote:

> When I came up from dinner today at about 25 to 1 we were running side by side with the *Olympic* about 60 or 70 yards from her. I sent the signalman of the watch aft to the colours. I heard the order given 'Steady on the *Edgar*' and heard it repeated. Then Lieut. Bashford came off the chart house and pointed out the *Edgar* to the helmsman. The *Edgar* was then on our port bow. I then directed my attention to the *Jupiter* in Stokes Bay for 3 or 4 minutes. The next order I heard was 'Port' followed by 'Hard a port' then the quartermaster reported the helm jambed and I saw the helmsman, quartermaster and Lieut. Bashford trying to turn the wheel. The next order was 'full speed astern' and we struck the *Olympic*. Just before this I noticed a chequered buoy which we passed on our starboard hand very close.

Able Seaman Alfred Crookham described noticing *Olympic* "off our port bow" at about 12:30pm. "She came towards us turned a buoy and steamed parallel to us about 100 yards. We were steaming together for about 5 minutes during which time she gained on us and gradually drew ahead. I then noticed our ship's head pay off to port and next moment she struck the *Olympic*. I saw 2 buoys pass close on our starboard hand shortly before the collision. I came down from aloft as we struck."

Lieutenant Aylen noted: "The actual position of the collision was not ascertainable owing to the rapid oscillation of the compass card, caused by the impact and the attraction of the moving iron of the ship." His written statement concluded: "I consider the SS *Olympic* to blame in not observing the Rule of the Road by not easing her engines or waiting till there was sufficient sea room to pass *Hawke*."

His colleague Lieutenant Geoffrey Bashford remembered *Hawke* being drawn into *Olympic*'s side, even as they tried so desperately to avoid a collision: "…The order was then given full speed astern both engines, the ship, however, continued to pay off rapidly to port as though the helm was hard a starboard. We struck the *Olympic* on her starboard quarter and orders were given to close W.T. [watertight] doors."

Petty Officer Ernest Hunt had been ordered by Bashford to take the helm.

> I took it and steadied the ship on her course and while I was looking ahead I noticed the *Olympic* apparently coming right across our port bow. Almost at the same instant I heard the Captain call down the voice pipe "What helm have you got on?" I sung out "port helm." Immediately the captain shouted "hard a port." I put the helm over and it jammed at fifteen degrees. I reported "helm jammed." The captain sung out "full speed astern both." Lieutenant Bashford, helmsman [Leading Seaman Henry Yeates] and myself tried to get the helm over but could not move it. The next thing was the collision. After the collision when the ship was stopped I managed to get the helm back amidships. During the time I had the wheel no starboard helm was given.

Commander Blunt's statement was the longest, as he explained that *Hawke* had been engaged in a "three-fifths power trial." He gave a dramatic account of the moments before the collision, and lost no time in placing blame on *Olympic*. *Hawke* had given *Olympic* as much room as possible. Shortly before the collision, *Hawke*'s bow began to veer to port, and he had demanded: "What are you doing? Port, port, hard aport!"

> Before the words were out of my mouth I realized the swerve was exceptional and ordered "Stop port [engine]; full astern starboard" and sprang for the ladder [to the lower bridge]. As I sung out the report came "helm jammed" whereupon I sprang down the ladder and putting the port telegraph myself to full astern ordered "full astern both." The suction of the *Olympic* was such that the *Hawke*'s port bow struck the *Olympic*'s starboard quarter crumpling the former and tearing a rent in the latter.

"In my opinion," Blunt concluded, "the collision was caused by the *Olympic* misjudging her turn round the Bramble Bank and thereby coming so close to the *Hawke* that as she forged ahead past her the suction due to her great mass drew the *Hawke* in on her. The *Hawke* could give no more room owing to the proximity of the Prince Consort Shoal."

"Generally speaking for two ships passing one another did you consider the *Olympic* was too close to you?" he was asked. "Considering her great bulk, yes, and consequent unhandiness. In fact I never liked her proximity the whole time, and I did my best to give her all the room possible."

His answer prompted the following exchange: "Have you any remarks to make as to how the Rule of the Road was observed or not observed by the *Hawke* and *Olympic*?" "Yes," he replied, as he added some important observations:

> When I first sighted the other ship they were absolutely on safe courses had they each continued their courses at the same speed. When I first saw the *Olympic* I was under the impression that she was going down through the Needles Channel and it was not till she sounded two blasts that I realized that she was going to the eastward, as she was then on starboard helm and having her starboard side to me, on a closing course I considered that under Article 19 of the 'Rules for the Prevention of Collisions at Sea' it was not my place to give way, and later when the turn of the *Olympic* was completed and she was in close proximity on my port hand I could hardly realize that she intended to cross my bow and take the channel to the south side of the Ryde Middle, when she had all the rest of the channel open to her. With reference to the *Olympic*'s turn round the Bramble Buoy she was followed some time after by the German liner *Konig Wilhelm* and I noticed that while we were lying at rest after the collision her own turn brought her a full half mile to the north of us although we were then lying further to the north than at the time of the collision.

If Blunt's observation was accurate, then that indicated *Olympic* could have given considerably more room to *Hawke* and that might even have saved the collision from happening at all. Asked if it was the case that "all alterations of course which you made during this time were away from the *Olympic* and calculated to clear her or give her more room?" he said, "Yes."

Under questioning, Lieutenant Aylen made the remarkable observation that "my notebook was knocked overboard by the collision." Consequently, he was unable to provide the exact "fix" he had taken for *Hawke*'s position before the collision. He confirmed his written statement when he said that "directly *Olympic* came up abreast the compass started oscillating." Just before the collision, *Hawke*'s compass was "spinning right round." At that time, *Hawke* was being drawn into *Olympic*'s side: "The ship did not stop slewing but continued more rapidly as time went on till we struck the *Olympic*. It was apparent it was actuated by some outside force. The swerve was very quick and no helm could have brought her round so quickly."

When Moore received the two-page "Finding of the Court," it read: "We are of the opinion that from the evidence heard that the *Olympic* alone is to blame." Commander Blunt appeared "to have done all in his power to give the *Olympic* as much room as possible, and was as close as he could be to his starboard side of the channel. We consider that he could not have done otherwise than he did and that he is in no way to blame."

Grant and Booty summarized *Olympic*'s responsibility:

> The *Olympic* came out of Southampton Water, and was throughout on the port hand of HMS *Hawke*. The *Olympic* should therefore have kept out of the way of the *Hawke*.

> The *Olympic* on ranging up abreast of the *Hawke* passed too close to her. The *Olympic*, though perhaps not the overtaking ship according to the definition laid down, had excess of speed over the *Hawke* and could have reduced speed to keep astern of her in the narrow channel, seeing that she was obliged by the Rule of the Road to keep out of the way. Instead of which she attempted to pass the *Hawke*.

From the naval authorities' perspective, their ship had not been at fault for the collision, which undoubtedly helped to relieve any embarrassment on the part of the Royal Navy.

However objective they had tried to be, unfortunately the very nature of the enquiry made it difficult to understand the broader picture. The version of events was given exclusively by naval personnel on board *Hawke*. No witnesses from *Olympic* were involved, and their perspective was entirely absent.

If the naval authorities felt they had an answer as to who was at fault, then the White Star Line understandably thought otherwise. Three days after the collision, Moore's receipt of the enquiry's findings was not the end of the matter, but the start; and it set the scene for over three years of legal proceedings during which the White Star Line continued to argue their case, and unearth new evidence which was not available to the naval enquiry.

Chapter III

TRIAL IN THE HIGH COURT OF JUSTICE

Mark Chirnside

The White Star Line lost no time in pursing their own argument. On the day after the collision, the company filed their own "statement of claim," delivered on 26 October 1911. They argued that the collision was "solely caused by the negligent navigation of the *Hawke*." They said that "a good lookout was not kept" by the cruiser; that she neglected to keep out of the way; that the cruiser's helm had been "improperly starboarded or her head was improperly allowed to come to port;" that her engines "were not eased or stopped or reversed in due time or at all;" that the cruiser "failed and neglected to indicate her maneuvers by the appropriate whistle signals;" and that she "improperly and at an improper time attempted to pass to the southward of the *Olympic*."

In opposition, the government made a case which was almost completely the opposite: that the collision was "caused solely by the negligent navigation of the *Olympic*;" that *Olympic* had not kept out of the way of *Hawke*; that she had come "too close to the *Hawke* and going at a speed which in the circumstances was excessive and improper;" "entering the Solent main channel at an improper time or in an improper manner;" "taking too wide a sweep round the West Bramble Buoy;" "not starboarding sufficiently or in due time;" "proceeding at an excessive speed;" and not reducing her speed or signaling properly her maneuvers.

Each statement of claim began with a summary of the moments leading up to the collision from each party's perspective. The government's summary included the assertion that "the *Olympic* with her starboard quarter struck the port side of the *Hawke*'s stem a heavy blow doing considerable damage…"

The White Star Line's own case against *Hawke* and the government's case against *Olympic* were heard together in the Probate, Divorce and Admiralty Division (Admiralty) of the High Court of Justice. Unlike the naval enquiry, which only took statements and testimony from *Hawke*'s crew, the court hearings would see both sides present their own evidence and argue their case that the other vessel was at fault:

The Oceanic Steam Navigation Company, Limited, Owners of the Steamship
Olympic, v. Commander William F. Blunt, of HM Cruiser Hawke: HMS Hawke

* * *

The Commissioners for Executing the Office of Lord High Admiral of the United
Kingdom v. Owners of Steamship Olympic: The Olympic
Before:
The Right Honourable Sir Samuel Evans, President
Assisted by Captain Thomson and Captain Crawford

The hearings began on Thursday, 16 November 1911. Mr. F. Laing, K.C., Mr. D. Stephens, Mr. H. C. S. Dumas, and Mr. L. F. C. Darby appeared for the Plaintiffs (the White Star Line); and Attorney-General Sir Rufus Isaacs, K.C., M.P., Mr. Butler Aspinall, K.C., Mr. A. D. Bateson, K.C., and Mr. C. Robertson Dunlop appeared for the Defendants (the government). As Attorney-General, Sir Rufus was a government minister, serving as the chief legal advisor of Liberal Prime Minister Herbert Asquith's administration.

In a nutshell, the White Star Line argued that under Article 24 of the Regulations for Preventing Collisions at Sea, *Hawke*'s duty was to keep out of the way of *Olympic*: "every vessel, overtaking any other, shall keep out of the way of the overtaken vessel." By contrast, the government's case was that, under Article 19 of the same regulations, "the vessel which has the other on her own starboard side shall keep out of the way of the other." In the White Star Line's argument, *Olympic* was being overtaken by *Hawke* on a parallel course, whereas the naval side argued that the two were on converging courses and therefore crossing vessels, which meant that *Olympic* needed to keep out of *Hawke*'s way because *Hawke* was on her starboard side. Although there were other breaches of the regulations, Articles 19 and 24 formed the key elements of the case.

The issues were not simple. Although *Hawke*'s speed had been maintained throughout, *Olympic*'s varied considerably as she made her maneuvers. Similarly, the two ships' courses varied in the moments preceding the collision, and witness testimony varied as to whether they were on parallel or converging courses.

Both sides tried to marshal the evidence that would support their own case, knowing that the opposing counsel would then be able to cross-examine their witnesses and try to find any holes in the testimony. Unlike a historical analysis, objectively analyzing all aspects of the collision, the duty of each side's legal team was to chose and present their evidence in such a way that it supported their own argument. Part of the process was in deciding which witnesses to call, and whether a particular witness's perspective would help or not.

The naval lawyers thought that Lieutenant Aylen's account proved their argument as to *Olympic*'s whereabouts when she was first seen: "Care will have to be taken to avoid the danger of the witnesses putting the *Olympic* too near the West Bramble Buoy before the *Hawke* had reached Egypt Point, as the result of the case depends so much upon the relative positions of the vessels when the *Hawke* altered course round Egypt Point and when the *Olympic* was close to the westward of West Bramble Buoy." A large scale chart and models would be prepared to help present the case: "The witnesses ought, if possible, to be in agreement about their estimates of distance between the two vessels…the witnesses…should be given the opportunities of making themselves familiar with the handling of models to avoid the mistakes which a witness frequently makes when asked in the witness box to show by the models the respective positions of two ships at a given moment." They felt their witnesses need to appear "in complete accord as to the orders given and the rapid sequence of events before the collision." Commander Blunt would "have to explain why he did not sound a port helm signal when he ported round Egypt Point, and later on when he ported near the East Council [*recte*: Conical] Buoy [also referred to as the Prince Consort Buoy]." Expert witnesses "who are likely to be able to explain the nature and effect of the forces which attract two vessels traveling at high speed in about the same direction" needed to be contacted quickly. Until they had been spoken to, it was difficult "to say who should be called without knowing what theories experts will advance, and whether their theories will agree, or will afford an explanation of what in fact happened…"

The White Star Line's legal team undoubtedly went through the same process before the case began.

The first witness called for the White Star Line was Captain Smith, and the hearings continued until 28 November 1911. Pilot George Bowyer followed, then *Olympic*'s officers, including Chief Officer Wilde and First Officer Murdoch, and witnesses from her engineering staff. Captain Pritchard, formerly of *Mauretania*, was called to testify about his own experience navigating the Cunarder, and Colonel Sexton White, general manager of Armstrong, Whitworth & Co.'s shipyard and an *Olympic* passenger, was seen as an independent observer who could help the White Star Line's case. Others testified as to the surveys of damage to *Olympic*, and what could be deduced from the physical evidence.

By the fourth day, the naval witnesses were being called, firstly Commander Blunt and then his other officers and crew. D. W. Taylor, a naval constructor for the United States, was also called to testify about the effects of hydrodynamic interaction between the two ships prior to the collision.

The two final days were taken up with closing arguments by the legal teams before Sir Samuel Evans. Laing had "a few words" to say about the question as to whether the *Hawke* had starboarded immediately before the collision.

> The eyewitnesses from my ship [*Olympic*] and the shore, all they can say is she [*Hawke*] looked as if she had starboarded, and beyond that I cannot go, but that there was something peculiar or unusual going on with the helm by the time when this vessel commenced this sheer, or whatever it was, is beyond doubt, because the helmsman was relieved and another helmsman took his place, and we had afterwards the jamming of the helm. Something was going on, at all events, quite unusual with the helm, and your Lordship will remember the shout of Captain Blunt, which he described as being in these words: "What are you doing? Port, hard a port," but Captain Blunt's recollection does not agree about this shout with Lieutenant Aylen's, and those who were on the bridge – their recollection of the shout was: "What are you doing with your helm?" That is quite another matter to "What are you doing? Port, hard a port." This vessel was a twin screw, and when this sheer was observed by Commander Blunt, undoubtedly the order was given, whether carried out effectively or not, is another thing. The first order that was given was: "Stop the port engine." I submit, stopping the port engine, if it was done, was not a seamanlike thing to do, that the port engine should have been kept going full speed ahead, and that the starboard engine should have been reversed if the proper maneuver had been carried out. Stopping the port engine would, I submit, be helping the cant towards the *Olympic*. The port engine was stopped, as we know by the evidence of the man who stopped it, and it was standing at stopped when the order to go astern both was given.

As for the theory about suction influencing *Hawke*, Laing tried to defuse it by saying "theory is one thing, practice is another, and this country has been engaged in shipping for a great many years." He continued: "I call attention with some confidence in this case to the evidence, not of the scientific experts, but the navigating experts, and the evidence I rely upon is Captain Smith, who had four voyages in the *Olympic*, and in the *Adriatic*, and all these large steamers of the White Star Line; Pilot Bowyer, who has taken the *Olympic* down these waters four times at least, and other large steamers; Captain Pritchard, the master of the *Mauretania*…" Eventually, he concluded:

> We say the whole question turns upon a question of fact, which was the overtaking vessel. If we establish the *Hawke* was the overtaking vessel, there is an end of all further discussion, because no inevitable accident is pleaded. It was her duty to keep out of the way, and she failed…
>
> Finally I have said that even assuming their case is absolutely true they might easily cut the cordian knot by easing up, and let this vessel get away – on their own story. They have no signal; at no time did they blow any signal, although they altered their course, according to them more than once, and if they saw this great vessel bearing down upon them, as their case is, it is an astonishing thing that they should have run on in the hope of squeezing past, and if they did it then they are entirely at fault for this collision.

Mr. Butler Aspinall was on his feet with the opposing case. He began by saying:

> We had hoped really in this case to have had the advantage of having the case presented to your Lordship by the Attorney-General, but unfortunately he has to be in another place protecting the interests if the country, and therefore the task falls upon me.

Aspinall then went on to summarize his case. He pointed out that just before the accident the White Star liner had been executing a difficult maneuver "for the purpose of getting into this narrow channel to the northward of the Isle of Wight, "not an easy operation."

> She was in the hands of an experienced pilot, but the man had no great experience of her [*Olympic*]; he had taken her out on four previous occasions, I suppose he had her in his charge on each occasion some few hours. It is not like a pilot working a ship in and out some hundred times or more. It is a difficult operation to take this big ship round, and it is a large turn that he is engaged in. I think I am right in saying something like 121 or 122 degrees; that would be an 11-point turn, and he is making the turn at considerable speed – in this present century speed goes on getting faster and faster, and, in the circumstances of this case, taking a vessel round at a speed, roughly speaking, it never fell to less than 10 knots…

In response to criticism from Laing about the brevity of entries in *Hawke*'s log, Aspinall suggested that more should have been written in *Olympic*'s log.

> First of all, nothing is said about passing the others' bows [*Hawke*]. He comes along, and gets into this other channel, and there are bows on his starboard hand, and not a word about it. Secondly, I would suggest one would have thought one would have found an entry here relating to the circumstances which led up to the collision, viz., as the ship was overtaking the other, and then passing her on the starboard quarter, she starboarded her helm and came into her. It is the barest statement of fact, merely that the collision happened, nothing more…One looks at the official log of the ship, which was also before the court: "Place of

occurrence by latitude and longitude," and all they say is: "Off Cowes, Isle of Wight." That is their official log description…

Aspinall pointed out that *Hawke* had achieved 17 knots "for the full power trials," which had been expected because she had not been in dry dock for some time. "Undoubtedly, the evidence we put forward as to our speed is accurate – records made at the time when one cannot say whether they are going to help us or benefit us for other documents drawn up and sent to the Admiralty – there it is in the log which is before the court, and results in giving us a speed of 15 knots." His argument as to speed showed *Hawke* was "always a crossing vessel." The eighth day was finished before he could finish his address, and so Butler Aspinall had to continue the following morning.

Aspinall dismissed the suggestion that *Hawke*'s helm had been starboarded prior to the collision:

> Now the suggestion is that we, coming up 300 yards away from this vessel, saw fit to starboard our helm. My friend [Mr. Laing] will not have suction, he says we starboarded. We were such a distance from him, that even if this force of suction did exist to some slight degree it could not exist under the circumstances of this case, and therefore the alternative is that we starboarded 300 yards away quite outside the sphere of any disturbance. He dealt quite lightly with that part of the case, and in one sentence. Now what is our evidence with regard to this? There is the evidence of Captain Blunt, who swears we never did starboard, of Mr. Aylen who says we did not, but he was not in such a position to speak to the matter as Captain Blunt. He certainly heard no order to starboard, and it is impossible to think it could have taken place without his noticing it. He is a navigator, it is his business to notice it, and then there is Mr. Bashford…He said the helm was under his observation, and it was never starboarded. There is evidence of the bluejacket to the same effect. It is a matter about which there cannot be any mistake…whether she answered her helm is just as simple a fact as whether I am standing in this Court or standing in the Divorce Court – there is no doubt about it. If it was starboarded there is very black testimony, and a conspiracy not to admit it…There is a suggestion which comes out; it was not pressed, but I must deal with it, that there was something wrong with the steering, and that possibly the helmsman made an error. I submit that this really is the weakest case that one could possibly have, because however chivalrous the King's officers may be, if the fault lay with the helmsman, Captain Blunt would not take it on his shoulders, and, extremely regretful as he may be that the thing happened, he must know that the helmsman had done it, and, of course, would say: "Why should I take the risk of it?" He would say at once it was the helmsman's fault.

Turning to the suction theory:

> In the last few years it has come into practice more than it did in the past. We are getting these Leviathans. It did not exist, perhaps, five years ago. We are getting greater speed on these vessels and less depth of water relatively to the shoals, and those are the elements which Professor Taylor claimed as being the factors which bring about the exercise of

these forces. Of course, in answer to that, the comment is going to be made that it is useless to call witnesses to prove a negative; but, apparently, this subject has been a matter of consideration amongst scientific gentlemen, and it is odd that we have seen nobody called from the other side to say, "Oh, yes; I have given this matter consideration, and I consider there is nothing in it."

Even if *Hawke* had been the overtaking vessel, Butler Aspinall argued that *Olympic* had no right to increase his speed. "What does he do? He puts his turbine into operation and goes on accelerating his speed. He introduces a new factor into force in his engine room, and introduces a new factor into his speed. That is wrong." Aspinall appealed to Evans, "…all I ask your Lordship to say is that the cause of this collision was a bungle made by the [*Olympic*'s] pilot in bringing his ship round in ignorance of the fact that we were there, that we had straightened on our course round this channel, that he was not conscious of the fact, that he did not get her quite round as he hoped, and the result of it was he ran into our water in the way I suggest."

Laing got up. "I have listened carefully to my friend's speech, and his summing up puts his case in a nutshell, and it is that the cause of the collision was a bungle of the pilot in ignorance of the position of the *Hawke*. All I can say in answer to that is, that you may search these seven volumes through, and you will not find a single question put to anybody on board of our ship in support of that view – not a single question." Supporting *Olympic*'s course, he said "the course was pleaded S. 59° E., and it was proved by the first witness, and never challenged till we hear these observations about it."

Laing returned to the "most unwarranted attack" Butler Aspinall had made "on the documents of my ship. He really, I think, said that my log books were not properly kept up and did not disclose the facts they ought to have disclosed with reference to this collision. I doubt if your Lordship has ever seen better-kept log books and more elaborate log books than have been produced by the *Olympic* in this case."

Attempting to answer the issue of whether they were crossing or overtaking (and overtaken) vessels, Laing stated:

> If the *Olympic* got into the strait of this channel with the *Hawke* behind her, as my original case is, they were certainly then overtaking ships undoubtedly. If the *Olympic* got into the channel abreast, so I gather, of the *Hawke*, which is the case on the other side, these vessels intending to go down South Ryde Middle, they probably never were on intersecting courses within the meaning of the rule, they never would intersect, they would proceed each down the channel going south and east would turn in the required position, and if they turned as required by the course they would never intersect at all. But these vessels were bound for the Nab. If they were both bound for the Nab through the same channel, they never were on intersecting courses, because the courses would never intersect; the *Hawke* would turn and proceed down the channel and the *Olympic* keep in a straight course down hers.

Answering Butler Aspinall's argument as to *Olympic* increasing her speed, Laing explained: "What she did was, coming round a corner her speed naturally falls off as she maneuvers her engines. When she get [sic] in the straight her speed naturally increased...She gets into the straight, and puts her engines full speed ahead. Can that be said to be an increase of speed, and a violation of Article 24 or 19? ...I submit certainly it is not a breach of the rule to regain your natural speed after you come round a corner, and get into the straight, especially if you are in the position of the overtaken ship, as my case is."

Samuel Evans handed down his judgment on 19 December 1911. The collision had been entirely unavoidable. "It ought not to have happened, but it did happen, and I have, to the best of my ability, to decide upon the evidence how and why it happened, and who are, or is, to be blamed for it, according to the law of Admiralty," Evans remarked as he summarized the collision and the resultant legal actions. His opening comments were lyrical:

> The collision took place on a fine day, not long after midday, in an open channel. The situation was free, and was not complicated by the presence, or navigation of any other vessels. One of the colliding vessels was the largest and finest product of the shipbuilding enterprise and skill of the first maritime nation of the world; the other was one of the protected cruisers of her navy. The contemplation of the calamity, and of the damage which resulted from it, cannot but produce a feeling of regret, and even a sense of pain.

Evans described *Olympic* as "a veritable 'Leviathan that maketh the deep to boil like a pot.'" He ran through the evidence about the courses, speeds and maneuvers of both ships leading up to the collision. The evidence from *Olympic* placed her further north than the accounts from *Hawke* which put the White Star liner further south into the channel. Evans concluded: "The explanation...is, I think, that the pilot with this huge vessel made too large and sweeping a turn round the Brambles." Worse still, "what tide there was – half a knot – would also tend to set her to the south." He also thought that she had been going faster than Laing had argued. *Hawke*'s speed could be ascertained more easily, and she was the slower vessel immediately prior to the collision.

> The *Hawke* was *not* [original *emphasis*] an overtaking vessel within the meaning of the rule.
> If either vessel was, it was the *Olympic*, which overtook the *Hawke*.
> I think that in approaching the place where the vessels collided, they were crossing vessels, and, as the *Olympic* had the *Hawke* on her starboard side, she ought to have got out of the way...

Evans did not accept the argument that *Hawke*'s helm had mistakenly been starboarded prior to the collision. Her officers and crew had testified to the contrary in court, and at the preceding naval investigation. Captain Smith's own phrase was invoked, when he had called it "an inconceivable maneuver."

> I am of the opinion that in the exceptional conditions which prevailed, the forces set up in the water are sufficient to account for the *Hawke* being carried towards the *Olympic* in a swerve that was beyond her control.

The *Olympic* had ample room and water in the channel to the northward. She came much too close to the cruiser on the south side of the channel. She did not take proper steps to keep out of the way. She might have averted the collision right up to the last if she had put her helm hard a starboard. Even when the pilot saw the *Hawke* come towards his vessel, he delayed action; and even when he took it, he ordered the helm hard a port, which was a very doubtful maneuver. In the agony of the situation, certain orders were given on the *Hawke*. They did not avail; but they were not wrong. In carrying them out the helm was jammed, but this was an accident for which no one is responsible, and which did not affect the collision.

Evans established:

1. That the *Olympic* has failed to establish her contention that the *Hawke* was an overtaking vessel bound to keep out of the way;
2. That the vessels were crossing vessels, and that the *Olympic* having the *Hawke* on her starboard side, should have kept out of the way of the *Hawke*;
3. That the *Hawke* was not to blame for what she did, or omitted to do;
4. That the cause of the collision was the faulty navigation of the *Olympic* by her pilot in going dangerously near the *Hawke*, and the non observance of the rule which required her to keep out of the way.

Although *Olympic* was held to blame by Evans, he noted that she was "in the charge of a duly licensed pilot in a compulsory pilotage district; that all the orders preceding the collision were given by the pilot; and that all his orders were properly and promptly obeyed." Evans mused, "it may be very desirable that the law as to the defense of compulsory pilotage should be altered…But it is for the legislature to make the law. My function is to declare and administer it as it now stands." Therefore, the White Star Line's defense on the grounds that their vessel was under compulsory pilotage succeeded.

Chapter IV

APPEALS AND JUDGMENTS

Mark Chirnside

The White Star Line did not accept that their vessel had been solely to blame for the collision. Although their defense of compulsory pilotage had succeeded, they wanted to clear their ship and the company from blame. They resolved to appeal the verdict, but the process was not a simple one. In order for them to introduce new evidence in appeal and thereby overturn the verdict of December 1911, they needed first to convince Lord Justices Vaughan Williams, Farwell and Kennedy in His Majesty's Court of Appeal. It was only then that they could proceed, and only if the appeal was successful that the original verdict would be overturned.

As the Appellants, *Olympic*'s owners were represented by Mr. Laing and Mr. Stephens; the Respondent, Commander Blunt, by Attorney General Sir Rufus Isaacs, Messrs Butler Aspinall, Bateson, and Robertson Dunlop. The initial hearing came on 13 March 1912, only a few months after the original verdict.

Laing began by summarizing the original case and findings, and he pointed out the problem of ascertaining the place of collision:

> The only people who could give evidence from my vessel about it were the master and the pilot, the collision having happened when the vessel is traveling at a speed of at least 16 knots an hour, six hundred yards a minute, and at a time when this vessel was full [sic] of passengers, and I will not say more than a moment of natural fear and excitement after this collision took place. The only evidence from the other ship was the evidence of the officer who said after the collision was over, and after the engines had been reversing for some time, and got to rest he took the cross bearings that were in the ship's logbook under the words "where struck" and afterwards altered to "mark the place of collision" where they finally marked it. The evidence as to this point therefore was not very clear or satisfactory.

His clients, the White Star Line, had considered sweeping the channel for any wreckage that would help to pinpoint the place of collision. Several pieces had been found, including part of *Hawke*'s forefoot, weighing seven and a half tons.

Butler Aspinall then stood up to appose the application to appeal. He recognized that new evidence could be admitted, but only "on special grounds," and he pressed the point that the White Star Line had gone to the original trial relying on the existing evidence. It had only been on 9 February 1912 that the dredging operations began.

Lord Justice Farwell asked Laing for clarification. Was establishing the point of collision for the purpose of proving which was the overtaking ship? Laing replied that the position north and south, "from shore to shore, is of importance to show she [*Hawke*] was not close to the south side as is said."

Laing also had his chance to explain some of the practical difficulties in arranging a search of the sea floor. "We had first to ascertain the depth of the water, and with divers and the sort of operation we were doing everything depends, of course, upon the weather, and we did not begin until February. It is said we might have begun in December. Everything depends on weather; tides and short tides and that sort of thing have to be taken into account, and the operations are going on at the present day." If the wreckage had been discovered "on the spot where my learned friend's clients placed the collision it would have been a very serious case for us, and we gave them notice that we were doing it so that they should be there to see precisely how the operations were conducted." He closed by asking:

> Are we seeking to unfairly put forward a matter which will tend to do injustice in this case? Can it be said that we are seeking to take advantage of this finding of this wreckage for some purpose which will be against the interests of justice? …When you find the evidence on both sides is of a nature which cannot necessarily be certain and you have offered to have the evidence of the finding of this wreck, which establishes at all events, the spot where this wreck was found, then I submit you ought to allow the evidence to be taken so that the matter may be discussed when this matter is discussed before the Court of Appeal.

The Lord Justices gave their judgment that afternoon. Vaughan Williams thought it was "a difficult case," but decided that the new evidence for the White Star Line could be submitted. Farwell came to the same conclusion, "although…with considerable hesitation, because I think, on the whole, there is more risk of our doing injustice by shutting out this evidence altogether than there is by our making an order for it to be tendered for reception by the court which hears the appeal." Kennedy agreed that the evidence could be submitted. "We are not considering the case of a new trial," he pointed out. "This is an application for leave to bring into existence evidence which the Court of Appeal may or may not admit at the time when it comes to ask that the evidence should be admitted on the hearing of the appeal."

Laing sought clarification about the evidence that the respondent could bring forward. Vaughan Williams explained that "It is not to be a fight merely over the position of the wreckage and what the effect of it is. The advisers of the *Hawke* will be entitled to call any evidence which they would have been entitled to call if this evidence [the discovery of the wreckage]…had been given at the [original] trial." Witnesses called before the court would be subjected to cross examination. Any evidence that Laing put forward could be challenged or refuted by Aspinall.

Joseph Gibney, a salvage contractor based in Liverpool, was called by Laing as the first witness on 15 April 1912. He confirmed he had been asked in early January 1912 to advise whether "there was any probability" of finding the wreckage. Gibney then described taking soundings in the channel, finding "rough sand and shingle." He engaged a diver, Peter McKenna, and hired a tug – *Adur*. On Friday 9 February 1912, they began their search, under the watch of HMS *Osprey*.

Edward Wilding testified on the third day, Wednesday, 17 April 1912. A week earlier, he might have been looking forward to the date and hearing about *Titanic*'s triumphant maiden voyage arrival in New York. Instead, he was in the uncomfortable position of having to testify as news of the *Titanic* disaster and its aftermath reached him. He confirmed he had inspected the wreckage found up to 10 April 1912, and that he had examined *Olympic* when she returned to Belfast the previous year. Harland & Wolff had sold the damaged plating to a scrap yard and "nearly all of it" had subsequently been recovered for examination. Wilding thought that the main wreckage now recovered had fallen from *Hawke* "at the conclusion of the third cut, and just as the next blade [of *Olympic*'s starboard propeller] was beginning the fourth cut on the body of the *Hawke*." His evidence emphasized the enormous stresses on *Olympic*'s structure when the *Hawke* came into contact with her starboard hull and wing propeller bossing, possibly jamming the starboard engine:

> I find some difficulty in saying that it absolutely did jam, but there was no question that the plating, when the vessel arrived in Belfast, was driven hard in, and the frames doubled up inside by pressure of the fore foot on the boss plating, and that the boss plating and framing had been driven down on a big loose coupling which was beneath them, and that the [*Olympic*'s starboard] engine, in its effort to go round, or to continue going round, when the pressure came on it, had torn and done very considerable damage to the framing inside the structure of the *Olympic*; and it is quite in my mind conceivable – although, of course, it is not certain – that that was sufficient to bring up the engine momentarily. Then, as the pressure of the *Hawke*'s fore foot was lifted off by her movement over the big propeller casting, that the engine was sufficiently free to be enabled to go on again. I do not think many people who have not been there, realize the enormous power that there is got from the steam pressure in these engines; they move comparatively slowly even when at full power, and the power behind them is, I think I am correct in stating, larger than the power behind the biggest rolling mills in the world. That is, the biggest mills that are used anywhere for the rolling of steel plates, as distinct from the forging of armor plates; consequently, the power that is available for doing damage is enormous, so that it is almost impossible to say that the comparatively modest damage, such as the damage on the boss plating, did bring up the propeller. But, allowing for the fact that the weight of the *Hawke*, the whole weight of the forward end…, was sitting momentarily on the loose coupling, it is at least conceivable that it was brought up there… I may say that as far as we could tell – we made some estimate of it – the starboard engine of the *Olympic*, when running at 64 revolutions, was probably giving something like 12,000 horsepower…

Frederick John Blake, the White Star Line's superintendent engineer at Southampton since 1907, was called. He described the operations and gave evidence as to the position where the "big piece, the fore foot" was found on Sunday 11 February 1912. The position had been taken onboard the tug, and then the party went onboard HMS *Dryad*, whose officers were in agreement. The next day, "we came out in the morning and the positions were then taken again."

> Mr. Laing: During the whole time you were there was there ever any dispute about position, or any difficulty about it at all?
>
> Mr. Blake: None whatever; there was a slight discrepancy between [Lieutenant] Smith and the naval gentlemen; just a few, which did not amount to anything. They said they were practically correct, practically the same.
>
> Mr. Laing: Was there anything worth taking notice of?
>
> Mr. Blake: No; what you would expect from two men doing the same thing.

During the fifth day's hearings, on 5 July 1912, questions raised by Mr. Bateson dismayed Mr. Laing. Colonel Hobart, a Lieutenant-Colonel in the Territorial Force and a holder of the Distinguished Service Order (DSO), was queried about what he had seen onboard the *Hythe* boat that left Southampton at 12:15pm on 10 April 1912. Hobart confirmed he had been watching the new *Titanic* "as she started from her berth in the new wet dock." Laing immediately objected.

> Mr. Bateson: We are proposing to prove that these large ships do affect other vessels when they are passing them and to give an instance which is well known as the *Titanic*.
>
> Mr. Laing: I can only protest, but it does seem monstrous that we should go into this question of suction.

Laing explained, "if you are going to call evidence about the *Titanic*, it means that I shall have to call evidence about the *Titanic* also to explain it. I know nothing about it, and I object to it." Bateson acquiesced, and did not question Colonel Hobart further, but hoped that he would be allowed to call it by the Court of Appeal.

On 5 April 1913, the company received the bad news. Vaughan Williams began by summarizing the case, noting that the finding of the wreckage had been admitted as evidence and that the justices had "satisfied ourselves that the search for the wreckage was not postponed by the *Olympic* taking their chance of winning their case independently of any search for wreckage." He went through all the arguments put forward and upheld the original judgment.

Kennedy acknowledged that "the case is difficult, owing to the conflict of testimony…but I have heard nothing which convinces me that, upon the evidence as it then stood, the judgment appealed against was wrong in its conclusion; and, subject to some qualifications…the reasoning upon which it was founded is reasoning from which I see no cause to dissent." He differed from the original judgment on one aspect:

> It is important to bear in mind that the burden of proving that the *Hawke* was an overtaking vessel lay upon the Plaintiffs [*Olympic*]. If they had made this out, I think that the *Hawke* must have been held to blame. It is clear to my mind that before the two vessels, after passing the Chequers Buoy, came into fatal proximity, she could have avoided any risk of collision by stopping or easing her engines; and if, as the new evidence shows, the *Hawke* must have been more near the mid channel, and therefore considerably further from the line of the buoys than her witnesses admit, I am by no means sure that she had not room to prevent

> the risk without a change of speed by a moderate porting of her helm before that point was reached. When it was reached she did port, but the action of the helm was ineffectual owing to the jamming of the gear…I cannot concur [with the original judgment]…that this jamming of the steering gear can be treated as "an accident for which no one is held responsible." It appears to me that the effect of the evidence of Captain Blunt is that the helm jammed through the negligent and unduly violent handling of the gear…
>
> In my judgment, therefore, this court is relieved from the necessity of considering what ought to have been the judgment of the court if the *Hawke* had been found to be at the material time in the position of an overtaking vessel under Article 24. The burden of proof lay upon the plaintiffs, and in my view that have failed to make out their case.

Kennedy thought *Olympic* "occasioned the collision by taking no step whatever to keep her out of the way of the *Hawke*, which was a crossing steam vessel on her starboard side," and asserted, "A very slight starboarding on the part of the *Olympic* almost up to the last moment would have prevented the collision, and there was ample room to the northward…"

Lord Justice Parker spoke about Pilot George Bowyer and how he had "misjudged the situation."

> From the first, the pilot seems to have misjudged the situation. He was aware of the presence of the *Hawke* in the channel, and appears to have made up his mind that the *Olympic* would come round into the channel far ahead of her. In this he entirely misjudged either the relative speeds of the two vessels or their distance from each other. His first error, no doubt, contributed to a second and more serious mistake. When the *Olympic* steadied on her course he entirely misjudged the bearing of the *Hawke*. He thought she was well abaft the beam, and, therefore, paid very little attention to her, it being, on that footing, her business to keep out of the way. He also misjudged his own position in the channel, which was, in fact, much more to the south than he supposed. He further misjudged the *Hawke*'s course, thinking it a parallel, whereas it was, in fact, a converging course. He thus failed to realize his duty to keep out of the way. Even when the *Hawke* commenced her swerve he delayed action til too late.
>
> The decision of the court…was, I think, right, and, notwithstanding the new evidence, ought, in my opinion, to be affirmed.

The only option for the White Star Line was to take their argument all the way to Britain's highest court, the House of Lords. As the upper house of the British Parliament, the House of Lords had seen some of its powers reduced following the rejection of the Liberal government's budget in 1909. The government brought in the Parliament Act in 1911 and, in effect, the upper house lost its right to veto money bills completely, as the elected House of Commons sought to assert its primacy over the upper house. However, it retained its function through the Law Lords as the final court of appeal in the justice system, until the creation of a Supreme Court in the United Kingdom in 2009.

By 9 November 1914, the final judgment was handed down. Almost three years had passed since the original verdict from December 1911. Lord Haldane, serving as Lord Chancellor since June 1912, outlined the appeal for the Lords. He explained that the additional information that had come to light since the original hearings required reviewing. Haldane had not been speaking for long before he dismissed the White Star Line's argument that *Hawke*'s helm had been mistakenly "starboarded just before the collision," the original president of the Admiralty Court and the Court of Appeal had both rejected the argument, and their findings "must, I think, be accepted as conclusive." He also pointed out that the "burden of making out their case" rested on *Olympic*'s owners and reviewed the well-rehearsed issues that made up the disagreements between both parties. New evidence relating to the placement of the navigating buoys, which had been marked inaccurately on the naval charts used in 1911, now put *Hawke* "considerably northwards" of her previous position in the channel. He thought the naval vessel must have been "sufficiently close to the *Olympic* just before the collision to render it possible that the force of interaction…was the real cause of the collision."

Unfortunately for *Olympic*'s case, he did not think the attention of the witnesses who had placed her on a parallel course with *Hawke* "was sufficiently concentrated on the point to make it quite reliable testimony as to the courses having been really parallel. Some of them, when pressed, were not prepared to pledge themselves in the witness box to exactitude." By contrast, Haldane found Commander Blunt and Lieutenant Aylen's statements "quite distinct" and reaffirmed the previous findings that "the two vessels were on intersecting courses, converging to the extent of 15 degrees, and were crossing vessels within the meaning of the rules." He also found that the evidence did not support the suggestion that *Hawke* was an overtaking vessel. "The average speed of the *Olympic* herself between the time when she steadied on her final course and the moment of impact was considerably in excess of the average speed of sixteen knots, and that she, therefore, could not have been overtaken by the *Hawke*." Her speed was taken at twelve knots at 12:43pm and "she would increase her speed to 20 knots in three or four minutes." Even if it had then taken five minutes to reach the place of collision (allowing for the ship's clocks recording minutes only and not showing seconds), then the average speed would have been fifteen knots:

> As her engines were only set at full speed after this interval commenced, she must have traveled at an increasing speed and gone faster during the latter part of the interval than during the earlier part. If the *Hawke* was behind her originally, she could never, having regard to the speed of the other vessel, have overtaken her, for a simple calculation shows that, in order to accomplish this, the speed of the *Hawke* would have had to have been 16.8 knots…

The failure to prove that the naval vessel had been an overtaking ship doomed the White Star Line's case:

> It seems to me that the real explanation of what happened is that her pilot thought that the *Olympic* would come round into the channel well ahead of the *Hawke*. He appears to have misapprehended the speeds of the two vessels and their relative positions. He seems to have thought that the

Hawke was abaft his beam when she was not, and that he himself was further north in the channel than he really was. He took the *Hawke* to be on a parallel instead of what was a converging course. As the result he did not discharge the duty which the Collision Rules imposed on him of keeping the *Olympic* out of her way.

"Whatever might be said against the view that the jamming of the helm was an accident for which no one could be held responsible, the point seems to me to be insufficient to affect the result of this case," he said. "Nor do I think it has been shown…that the *Hawke* ought, according to the rules of good seamanship, to have ported before reaching the Chequers Buoy, or that the pilot of the *Olympic* was at liberty to or did in fact assume that she would do so." Lords Atkinson and Shaw concurred. The House of Lords dismissed the appeal with costs.

Chapter V

AN *OLYMPIC* TALE

Samuel Halpern

The location in the channel where *Hawke* struck *Olympic* was never really agreed to at the High Court of Justice trial that was held in November 1911. The diagram below (Fig. 5-01) shows the location put down on the chart for the collision by the White Star Line (WSL) during the preliminaries as well as the locations put down for the collision during the trial by Captain Smith, the pilot George Bowyer, Col. Sexton White (a passenger witness for the WSL), and Lt. Aylen (*Hawke*'s navigation officer). In addition to these, we also show the point put down on the chart by Lt. Aylen for a fix that was taken after *Hawke* came to a stop following the collision, the point put down by Captain Smith for where *Olympic* steadied on her course following the turn around the West Bramble buoy, and the place put down by Captain Smith as to where *Hawke* was at the time *Olympic* steadied on her new course.

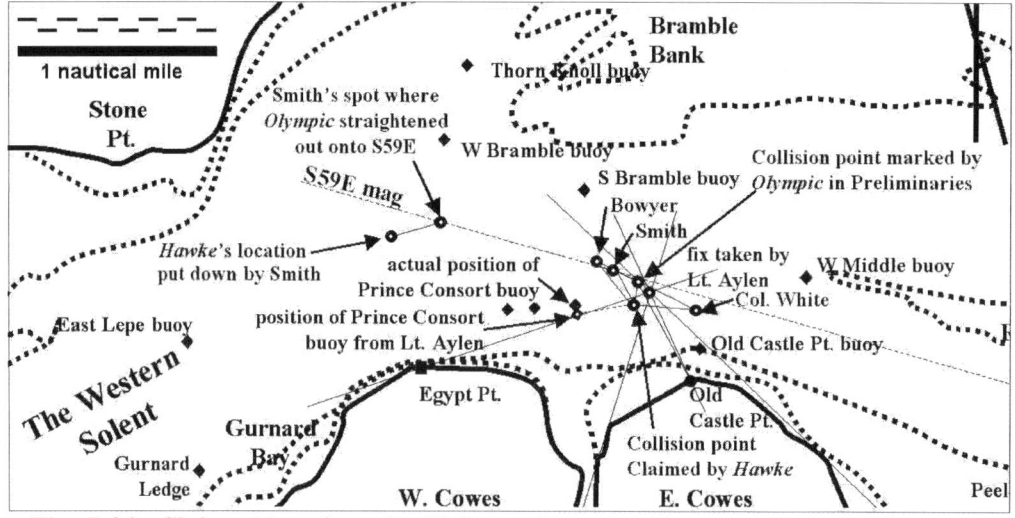

Fig. 5-01 **Claimed location of collision point according to several eyewitnesses.**

All these marked positions were subjective estimates except for the fix taken by Lt. Aylen after the collision. That was in reference to bearings that were taken off four specific landmarks. Those bearing lines are also reproduced on the chart above.[1] We also know that the actual collision point had be very close to that fix as *Hawke* could not have moved very far from the actual point of collision when she finally came to a stop.

Another point that should be considered is that the position of the Prince Consort buoy on the Admiralty charts in use at the time was about 70 yards too far south of where the buoy actually was located in 1911. The place of collision put down by Lt. Aylen was in reference to the position of that buoy. He said the collision happened S87E (magnetic) [077° T] and 3 cables length from the Prince Consort buoy. In reality, his collision position should have been put down about 70 yards further northward relative to the landmarks on the chart because of that error. This would have brought it somewhat closer to the point put down by the WSL in the preliminaries.

As far as the other points that we show on the chart, those attributed to Smith, Bowyer and White were all marked off by reference to the point put down on the government chart by the WSL in the preliminaries. The exact position of the WSL collision point was marked by a small circle on the government chart and identified by the words "Place of Collision according to Olympic." That point was at a measured distance of 5.6 cables on a line of bearing 29° west of true north [331° T] taken from the bath house located on Old Castle Point which was also shown on the chart. Also put down on the government chart was the point of the fix taken by Lt. Aylen. This was marked by a small circle labeled "12.50," the time the fix was taken.

A copy of the government chart showing these points was included in a March 1912 discussion article that appeared in Vol. 38 of the *US Naval Institute Proceedings*. Only a partial scan taken from that chart is available, and is shown below in Figure 5-02. Added to this partial scan of the government chart are the locations of the Prince Consort buoy (7 cables 289°T) and the West Middle buoy (6 cables 55.5°T) from the Old Castle Point buoy as reported in *The Channel Pilot* at the time.

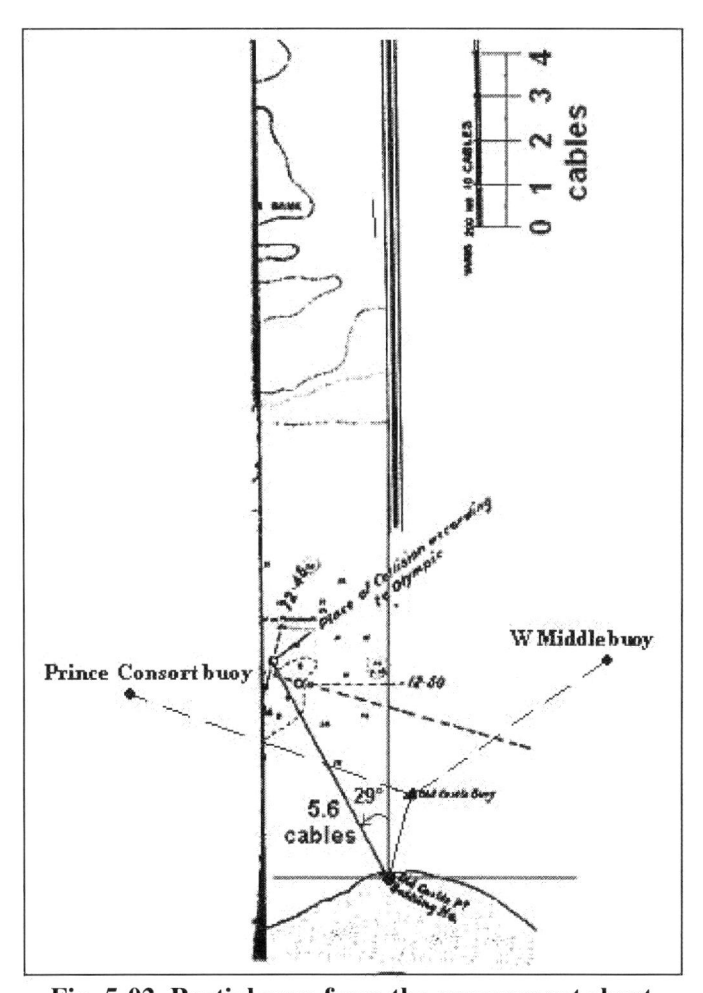

Fig. 5-02 Partial scan from the government chart.

It should be noted that the collision point put down on the government chart by Captain Smith was measured at 260 yards (1.3 cables) NW magnetic [299° T] of the WSL point, Bowyer's collision point was 420 yards (2.1 cables) NW magnetic [299° T] of the WSL point, and Col. White's point was 650 yards (3.25 cables) SE magnetic [119° T] of the WSL point. Relative to the collision point put down by Lt. Aylen, Captain Smith's point was 400 yards (2 cables) N by W magnetic [333° T] from Aylen's.[2]

The place on the chart marked by Captain Smith where *Olympic* steadied on her course of S59E measures about 4 cables south of the West Bramble buoy. Pilot George Bowyer said that *Olympic* was about 2 to 3 ship lengths south of the buoy when her swing was checked after rounding the buoy. *Olympic* was almost 1 ½ cables in overall length, and a distance of 4 cables from the buoy corresponds to just over 2 ½ *Olympic* ship lengths, thus being consistent with what Bowyer said. But the time recorded in the scrap log had the West Bramble buoy abeam at 12:42. The time put down for when *Olympic* steadied on her course of S59E was 12:43, just one minute later. According to both Smith and Bowyer, *Olympic* passed about a cable's length off the buoy, and when the buoy was abeam, her port engine, which had been put slow-ahead at 12:40 when *Olympic* passed the Thorn Knoll buoy, was stopped and put full-astern to sharpen the turn around the Bramble.[3] After *Olympic* steadied on S59E, her port engine was stopped again and then put full-ahead, and by 12:44 the turbine engine was connected back up. It should be noted that for *Olympic* to travel about 4 cables south of the buoy in one minute of time (from 12:42 to 12:43) she would have to have been going at a speed of 24 knots, which was not possible. It is more likely that it was closer to 12:44 when she was steadied, the time recorded when the turbine was put back on line.

Overall, the measured distance covered by *Olympic* from the North Thorn buoy (which was passed at 12:37) to the point of collision (at 12:46) as marked on the chart by the WSL was about 25 cables. The time interval taken from the wheelhouse clock was 9 minutes, but it could have been closer to 10 minutes because of the 1 minute uncertainty caused by how the clock incremented. This implies that *Olympic* had to average from 15.0 to 16.7 knots to cover the 2.5 nautical miles from the North Thorn to the place of collision as put down by the WSL.

But we also know that *Olympic* was accelerating to her full ahead speed for restricted waters after turning the Calshot Spit buoy (which was passed at 12:34) as she headed down the Thorn Channel on a heading of S65W magnetic [229° T]. At the Thorn Knoll buoy her port engine was put to slow-ahead, the turbine engine stopped, and her helm put "starboard easy" to turn the ship for the West Bramble buoy. At the West Bramble buoy the port engine was stopped, then placed half-astern, followed by full-astern, and her helm put hard-astarboard to sharpen the turn around the buoy.

Over a measured distance of 19 ½ cables between the Thorn Knoll buoy (which was passed at 12:40) to the place of collision (at 12:46) as marked on the chart by the WSL, *Olympic* had to average from a minimum of 16.7 to a maximum of 19.5 knots. Even though we were told by Captain Smith and the pilot George Bowyer that she had slowed down to about 11 or 12 knots coming out of the turn around the West Bramble buoy, for *Olympic* to average between 16.7 to 19.5 knots between Thorn Knoll and place of collision as marked by the WSL, her speed had to be coming close to 20 knots when she was struck by *Hawke*.[4] This implies that *Olympic* was probably going at a speed that was somewhat greater than the claimed 11 or 12 knots when coming out of the turn around the buoy.

As far as the position of *Hawke* at the time *Olympic* steadied on her course after turning around the West Bramble buoy, Captain Smith placed her on the chart at a position about 1,330 yards (6.65 cables) to the north magnetic [344° T] of Egypt Point, a prominent landmark and lighthouse on the northern shoreline of West Cowes.[5] This would make it consistent with the claim that *Hawke* was then 2 to 3 points on *Olympic*'s starboard quarter and about ¼ of a mile back at that time. But according to *Olympic*'s pilot George Bowyer, *Hawke* was coming up the western Solent on a course of N76E magnetic [060° T] when he ordered two blasts be sounded on *Olympic*'s whistles to let *Hawke* know that he was taking the turn around the buoy to enter the east Solent. *Olympic* was then 2/3 the distance down the channel from the Thorn Knoll buoy to the West Bramble buoy, a position also observed and confirmed by *Hawke*'s Lt. Aylen when those two steam whistle blasts were seen from *Hawke*. Bowyer said that *Hawke* was then about 1 ½ miles away in mid-channel abreast of Gurnard Bay. He also said "she was as near the [East] Lepe buoy as she was the Gurnard [Ledge buoy]" when he saw her coming up the channel. The distance between these two buoys was about 6 cables, and *Hawke* would have passed Egypt Point about 3 ½ cables off coming up on that particular courseline.

The evidence given by *Hawke*'s officers was that she was coming up on a heading of N77E magnetic [061° T] and passed about 3 ½ cables off Egypt Point when she was turned onto a heading of S74E magnetic [090° T] to parallel the three buoys outside of Cowes harbor. But if the position put down on the chart by Captain Smith as to where *Hawke* was when *Olympic* straightened out on her course of S59E magnetic was close to being correct, it would mean that *Hawke* was coming up the Solent on a line that would have passed within just a few yards of the East Lepe buoy and about 6 ½ cables off Egypt Point. That is inconsistent with what Bowyer observed and what *Hawke*'s Commander Blunt and Lt. Aylen had claimed. It is also inconsistent with what Henry Lashmar, a witness for the White Star line, claimed he saw from his moored yacht *Bellinda* off of Cowes Roads. Lashmar estimated that *Hawke* was about mid way between the East Lepe buoy and the shoreline on the Isle of Wight when he saw her coming up to Egypt Point. All of these observations are shown in Figure 5-03 that follows.

The testimony of witnesses for *Olympic* was suspiciously similar in detail regarding the position of *Hawke* after *Olympic* completed her turn around the West Bramble buoy. Captain Smith originally said that he thought *Hawke* was about ½ mile back when he saw her 2 ½ points on his starboard quarter as he turned around to look after *Olympic* had steadied on her course. Later he said she might have been closer than that based on how long it took for *Hawke* to come up abreast of *Olympic*'s bridge. He first saw *Hawke* when *Olympic* was heading down the Thorn channel on a heading of S65W magnet [229°T] approaching the North Thorn buoy, and *Hawke* was then from ½ to 1 point on *Olympic*'s port bow and about 3 to 4 miles away.

Pilot George Bowyer claimed that he first saw *Hawke* 3 to 4 miles away about 1 point on *Olympic*'s port bow when *Olympic* was abreast of the North Thorn buoy. As we have seen, he ordered two blasts blown on *Olympic*'s whistles when *Olympic* was 2/3 the distance down from the Thorn Knoll buoy to the West Bramble buoy to tell *Hawke* that *Olympic* was taking a turn to port to round the Bramble, and that *Hawke* was then about 1 ½ miles away between the East Lepe and Gurnard Ledge buoys coming up the West Channel. Bowyer also said that he next noticed *Hawke* again after *Olympic*'s turn around the buoy was completed when she was spotted 2 to 3 points on *Olympic*'s starboard quarter and ¼ mile back from where he stood on the bridge. This would put her about a cable length back from *Olympic*'s stern.

Bowyer also thought that *Hawke* was steering about E by S magnetic (about S79E magnetic) when she was ¼ mile astern, and would have crossed *Olympic*'s stern if she would have held that course. However, he also agreed that *Hawke* may have been steering S74E as suggested by counsel for *Hawke*. The next time he saw *Hawke* was when her stem was coming up to *Olympic*'s stern, and then she was on what seemed to be a parallel course to *Olympic* at a distance of about 2 cables apart. The next time Bowyer saw *Hawke* was when her stem came up to *Olympic*'s bridge just before she started to drop back and swing to port. He estimated that *Hawke* was then about 1 ½ cables off when she was abreast *Olympic*'s bridge.

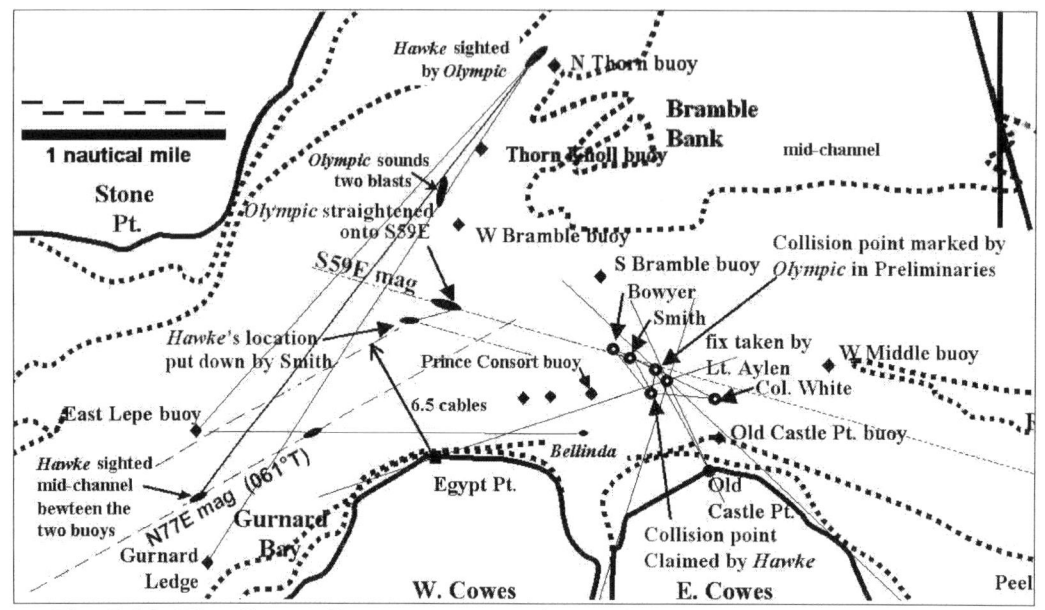

Fig. 5-03 Pilot George Bowyer saw *Hawke* coming up equidistant between the East Lepe and Gurnard Ledge buoys.

Olympic's sixth officer Harold Holehouse, who was stationed on the bridge recording events and taking the time from the wheelhouse clock, saw *Hawke* just before he was ordered by Bowyer to sound two blasts on *Olympic*'s whistles. He said *Hawke* was then about 1 to 2 miles away and to the westward of Egypt Point bearing a little on the starboard bow. He also said that he helped steady *Olympic* on her course after the turn around the West Bramble by calling out the heading (S64E) on the steering compass on the bridge when the fifth officer, Adolphus Tulloch, at the standard compass amidships, rung the on-course (three-bell) signal. After steadying *Olympic*, he noticed *Hawke* about 3 points on the starboard quarter and ¼ to ½ mile back. Interestingly, Holehouse said he did not actually take note of the time when *Olympic* actually steadied on her course, but formed "only a rough estimate" that the ship steadied "about a minute later after the Bramble Buoy was bearing abeam." The time the buoy was abeam was put down in the scrap log as 12:42, and time that the ship was steadied was put down as 12:43.

Adolphus Tulloch, *Olympic*'s fifth officer stationed on the amidships compass platform, testified that he first noticed *Hawke* about 2 miles away off *Olympic*'s starboard bow just after *Olympic*'s whistles were blown. He said *Hawke* had her port bow a little opened up to *Olympic* at that time. He also said that that *Olympic*'s course headings was given to him before he went to the platform after the ship started out from Southampton. He signaled 3 bells on the push-bell when he saw the ship was on her preset course of S59E by standard compass following the turn around buoy.[6] The next time he saw *Hawke* was just after he steadied the ship, about 1 ½ to 2 minutes before she came abeam of *Olympic* on a parallel course about 1 ½ cables apart from *Olympic*'s. The next time he noticed *Hawke* is when her stem was abreast of *Olympic*'s bridge, and then he saw her drop back, turn in toward *Olympic*, and then strike *Olympic* at what appeared to be a right angle blow.

David Alexander, *Olympic*'s fourth officer working the engine telegraphs on the bridge, said he first saw *Hawke* off *Olympic*'s starboard bow just after *Olympic* passed the Thorn Knoll buoy. He said she was then between Gurnard Head and Egypt Point and appeared to be about 2 miles away. The next time he saw *Hawke* was after *Olympic*'s engines were put full ahead after turning the Bramble. He said he turned around to look for no particular reason, and saw *Hawke* about 2 to 3 points on the starboard quarter and about ¼ mile back steering a parallel course to *Olympic*. The next time he noticed *Hawke* again was when her stem came up to *Olympic*'s bridge. He said she was about "a cable and a half to 2 cables" off. When she came up opposite *Olympic*'s bridge he rang the after bridge for them to dip the ensign, and saw *Hawke* dip her ensign and raise it again. He then rang aft for them to raise *Olympic*'s ensign as *Hawke* dropped astern. The next thing he heard was Captain Smith telling Bowyer that she was coming into them, and then he turned and noticed *Hawke* swinging under what appeared to be starboard helm. The next thing he heard was Bowyer ordering him to stop the engines and shouting to the helmsman "hard aport." He said he signaled "stop" just before *Hawke* struck.

William Murdoch, *Olympic*'s first officer, was on the after end of the ship when he heard 2 blasts from *Olympic*'s whistles. He then looked ahead and saw *Hawke* "coming along the starboard bow then…probably 3 miles [away]." The next time he took particular notice of *Hawke* was after *Olympic* steadied on her course to take the middle of the channel south of the Ryde Middle. He said *Hawke* appeared to be 3 points on the starboard quarter nearly ¼ mile back. Before that, he said that he could see his ship swinging past *Hawke* as the cruiser was coming up and getting on *Olympic*'s starboard quarter, but had not paid "particular attention to her" during the time *Olympic* was swinging. After noticing *Hawke* about 3 points on the starboard quarter after *Olympic* steadied, he left the poop to go to the aft end of the boat deck where he noticed *Hawke* coming up on a parallel course about 1,000 feet laterally from *Olympic*. He was on the port side of the boat deck when he saw the ensign dipped, and was headed back to the poop deck when *Hawke* struck. He did not witness the collision.

Henry Wilde, *Olympic*'s chief officer, was stationed on the forecastle head when he saw the cruiser about ½ point off *Olympic*'s port bow about 3 to 3 ½ miles away and "perhaps half a mile" to the westward of Gurnard Head. *Olympic* was then about half way between the Calshot Spit buoy and the North Thorn buoy. As they got down to the Bramble he heard 2 blasts from *Olympic*'s whistles as his ship took the turn, and later noticed *Hawke* again after his ship steadied on course when he got the No Mans Land Fort a little on his starboard bow. He claimed that *Hawke* was then 3 points on their starboard quarter and 2 cables [0.2 miles] astern overtaking *Olympic* on a course that might have been just "a little more to the north than [the course that] we were [on]."

Wilde thought that *Hawke* was "gaining fast" (3 or 4 knots) on *Olympic*, and the lateral distance between ships was about 1 ½ cables as *Hawke* continued to come up until her stem was abreast *Olympic*'s bridge, or a little aft. He then noticed *Hawke* suddenly swing toward *Olympic* as if under starboard helm and strike his ship aft at nearly a right angle. He also said he saw *Hawke* heel over heavily to starboard after she struck. He thought *Olympic* was going about 11 or 12 knots when she steadied on her course, and about 15 knots when *Hawke* struck.

Robert Hume, *Olympic*'s second officer, was in the crow's nest along with two lookouts when he spotted *Hawke* about a point to port and 3 ½ to 4 miles away to the west of Gurnard Head. *Olympic* had just rounded the Calshot Spit approaching the North Thorn buoy at that time. When *Olympic* was off the Thorn Knoll buoy, just before she started a turn to port to head down to the West Bramble buoy, he estimated that *Hawke* was about 1 ¾ miles away. When the 2 blasts of *Olympic*'s whistles were blown, he said that *Hawke* was about 1 ½ miles away and about 3 points on *Olympic*'s starboard bow west of Egypt Point. Under cross-examination, Hume said *Hawke* was "nearly a mile" away when those two blasts were given.[7] After *Olympic* steadied on her course following the turn around the Bramble, *Hawke* was ¼ mile astern and 3 points on *Olympic*'s starboard quarter on a parallel course, and later put her about 800 to 1,000 feet abreast of *Olympic* before she started to drop astern and turn into *Olympic*. He thought *Hawke* was about abeam of *Olympic*'s second funnel when she started to turn in and strike *Olympic* at what appeared to be a right angle blow. He also agreed that there was no particular reason why, being in the crow's nest, he decided to look aft just after his ship steadied on her course after completing the turn around the Bramble.

What is interesting and somewhat surprising about all these observations is that between the time that 2 whistles were sounded as *Olympic* approached the West Bramble buoy and when she was steadied onto her S59E courseline, *Hawke* was not taken under any particular notice by any of these officers, her captain or her pilot. Yet the testimony from *Olympic*'s officers put *Hawke* anywhere from a minimum of 1 mile (Hume), to 1 ½ miles (Bowyer and Holehouse), to 2 miles (Tullouch), to a maximum of 3 miles (Murdoch) from *Olympic* when those 2 whistles blasts were sounded as they all took particular notice of the cruiser for whom the signal was intended. Then the next time any of them took particular notice of *Hawke* was after *Olympic* steadied onto S59E, all saying that *Hawke* was from 2 to 3 points on *Olympic*'s starboard quarter and about ¼ to ½ mile back. These same officers also claimed that *Hawke* was running on what appeared to be a parallel course to that of *Olympic* soon after *Olympic* had completed her turn around the West Bramble buoy. The separation between the two parallel courses was claimed to be about 1 ½ cables (about 900 feet). Then, according to these officers, *Hawke* was seen to come up to a point where her stem was directly abeam *Olympic*'s bridge before she started to drop back as *Olympic* continued to accelerate ahead. *Hawke* then swerved toward *Olympic* as if her helm were put hard-astarboard and struck *Olympic* about 90 feet ahead of her stern at what appeared to be a right angle blow.

From the evidence put on a chart by E. J. Smith, *Olympic*'s captain, the distance between the point where *Olympic* had steadied and the point where the collision took place measured 1,770 yards, or 5,310 feet (8.73 cables).[8] The time claimed for when *Olympic* steadied on her course of S59E was 12:43. The time put down in the scrap log for the collision was 12:46.

The time of events recorded on the bridge by *Olympic*'s sixth officer Harold Holehouse was taken from *Olympic*'s wheelhouse clock. This clock, one of several slave clocks driven by a master clock in the chart room, incremented by minutes only, thus producing an uncertainty that could be as much as 1 minute between readings.

What we wanted to do is independently analyze the encounter based on these claims. To do so we need to get the total distance traveled by *Hawke* from time she was allegedly sighted about ¼ mile aft to the moment of collision. We know the distance traveled by *Olympic* was claimed to be about 1,770 yards over that time, and the time interval had to be somewhere between 3 and 4 minutes according to time taken from the wheelhouse clock.

Olympic's overall length was just over 882 feet, and *Hawke* struck *Olympic* just aft of her after well deck about 90 feet ahead of her stern. This is a point about 350 feet abaft *Olympic*'s amidships point, or about 600 feet aft of *Olympic*'s forebridge, which itself was about 190 feet aft of *Olympic*'s stem. *Hawke*'s turn into *Olympic* was about a quarter of a circle since she appeared to strike at nearly a right angle, and since it was claimed that the courses were separated by about 900 feet, that implies that *Hawke* traveled *at least* 1,415 feet over that quarter of a circle before striking *Olympic*.[9]

The details of this collision scenario based on these observations and claims are shown in Figure 5-04 below.

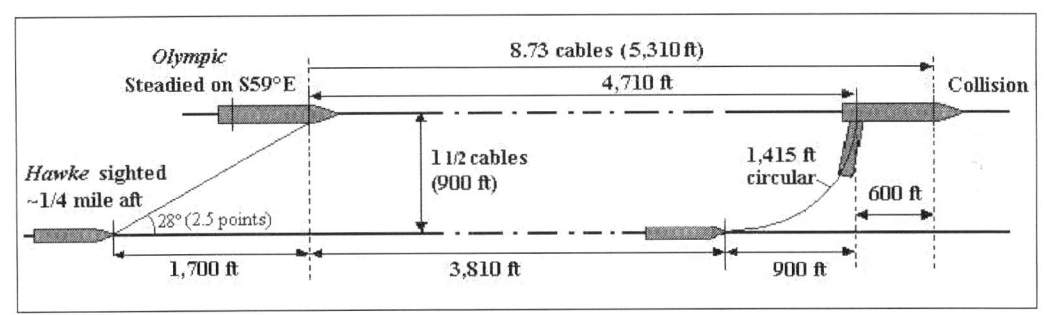

Fig. 5-04 Analysis of collision according to story of *Olympic*'s officers.

If we add up all the distance segments that *Hawke* had to travel before striking *Olympic*, we find that the total distance *Hawke* had to travel in time T was:

$$D_H = 1,700 + (5,310 - 600 - 900) + 1,415$$
$$D_H = 1,700 + 3,810 + 1,415$$
$$D_H = 6,925 \text{ ft}$$

In the same time interval, T, we were told that *Olympic* traveled a distance of 1,770 yards, or:

$$D_O = 5,310 \text{ ft}$$

To get the *average* speed for each ship in feet per minute we just have to divide these distances by the time interval involved, T, which was either a minimum of 3 minutes or a maximum of 4 minutes. Then, to get the average speed in knots, we just divide those speeds by 100 ft/min per knot. The results are:

For *Hawke*: $S_H = 23.1$ knots using T = 3 min.; or $S_H = 17.3$ knots using T = 4 min.

For *Olympic*: $S_O = 17.7$ knots using T = 3 min.; or $S_O = 13.3$ knots using T = 4 min.

An average speed close to 13 ½ knots for *Olympic* is not inconsistent with the claim by both Captain Smith and the pilot George Bowyer that *Olympic* was making 11 or 12 knots coming out of the turn around the West Bramble buoy and then accelerated to about 15 or 16 knots by the time *Hawke* struck. But that would mean that the time interval was closer to an elapsed time of 4 minutes, and that *Hawke* had to be making an average speed of about 17 knots for this scenario to play out as claimed.[10] However, evidence was presented during the inquiry that *Hawke* was going no more than about 15 knots all the time.

Between 7:30 and 11:30am, *Hawke* was engaged in a full power trial under natural draft (4/5 of forced draft power), and from 11:30am up to the time of the accident, *Hawke* was engaged in a 3/5 power trial also under natural draft conditions. Under the full power trial she was carrying 92 revolutions per minute on her propellers and making about 17 knots, while under the 3/5 power trial her revolutions were down to 82 per minute and she was making just over 15 knots.[11]

Another point to consider is that almost all eyewitnesses called on behalf of *Olympic* said that *Hawke* dropped back to a point about amidships of *Olympic*, between her second and third funnels, as *Olympic* was pulling ahead when *Hawke* first started to turn into *Olympic* as if under starboard helm. At the start of the turn the two ships were claimed to be about 1 ½ cables, or about 900 feet apart. We have just seen that *Hawke* had to travel over a circular distance of *at least* 1,415 feet for her to strike *Olympic* at nearly a right angle. Since *Hawke* struck *Olympic* about 350 feet aft of amidships, *Olympic* had to move forward a total of 900 feet plus 350 feet, or 1,250 feet during that time. Taking the ratio of these two travel distances implies that *Olympic* was going at a speed of only 88% of that of *Hawke* for this story to play out.[12] This is inconsistent with the claim of both sides that *Olympic* was going faster than *Hawke* when the swerve started, which is why *Hawke* appeared to drop back in the first place. The details of this can be seen in Figure 5-05 below.

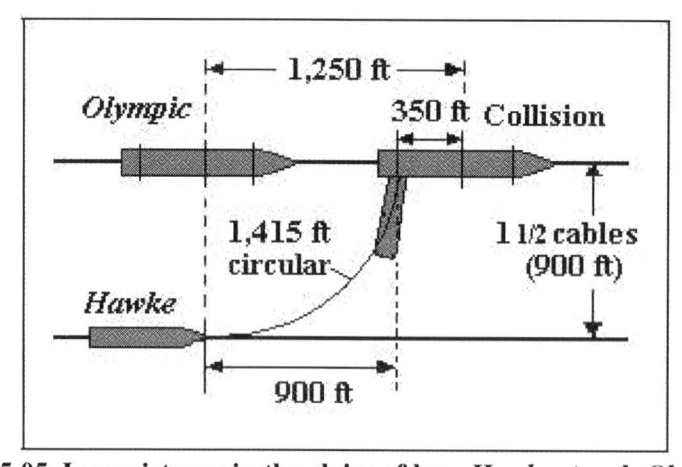

Fig. 5-05 Inconsistency in the claim of how *Hawke* struck *Olympic*.

It is expected that eyewitness accounts would differ somewhat from each other when it comes to specific subjective observations such as distances, bearings and time intervals. Yet, suspiciously, there was a great deal of similarity in the testimony for *Olympic* when it came to where *Hawke* was after *Olympic* steadied onto her course after turning around the West Bramble buoy, and that *Hawke* was then gaining on *Olympic*.

Counsel for *Olympic* placed a great amount of emphases on these observations during closing arguments. By doing so, *Hawke* was put in the precarious position of an overtaking vessel. Therefore, according to Article 24 in the Regulations for Preventing Collisions at Sea that were in effect at the time, it was *Hawke*'s duty to keep out of the way of *Olympic* because she was coming up from more than two points abaft *Olympic*'s beam:

> ARTICLE 24.
>
> Notwithstanding anything contained in these Rules, every vessel, overtaking any other, shall keep out of the way of the overtaken vessel.
>
> Every vessel coming up with another vessel from any direction more than two points abaft her beam, i.e., in such a position, with reference to the vessel which she is overtaking, that at night she would be unable to see either of that vessel's side-lights, shall be deemed to be an overtaking vessel; and no subsequent alteration of the bearing between the two vessels shall make the overtaking vessel a crossing vessel within the meaning of these Rules, or relieve her of the duty of keeping clear of the overtaken vessel until she is finally past and clear.
>
> As by day the overtaking vessel cannot always know with certainty whether she is forward of or abaft this direction from the other vessel, she should, if in doubt, assume that she is an overtaking vessel and keep out of the way.

Fig. 5-06 Article 24 from the Regulations for Preventing Collisions at Sea.

In addition to claiming that *Hawke* was in violation of Article 24, counsel for *Olympic* also claimed that *Hawke* was in violation of Articles 28 and 29.

> ARTICLE 28.
>
> The words "short blast" used in this Article shall mean a blast of about one second's duration.
>
> When vessels are in sight of one another, a steam vessel under way, in taking any course authorised or required by these Rules, shall indicate that course by the following signals on her whistle or siren, viz.:—
>
> > One short blast to mean, "I am directing my course to starboard."
> >
> > Two short blasts to mean, "I am directing my course to port."
> >
> > Three short blasts to mean, "My engines are going full speed astern."

Fig. 5-07 Article 28 from the Regulations for Preventing Collisions at Sea.

Olympic had indicated her intention to round the West Bramble buoy to take the East Channel by signaling two short blasts on her steam whistles when she was 2/3 the distance down between the Thorn Knoll and West Bramble buoys. *Hawke* never signaled her intention as to which way she was heading. However, coming up the West Solent it was assumed that *Hawke* would take a turn to head eastward, into the East Solent. Pilot George Bowyer said that he thought *Hawke* was going to take the channel north of the Ryde Middle when he saw her ¼ mile back on *Olympic*'s starboard quarter. He based that assumption on the apparent course that *Hawke* was steering at that time, which he said was about "E by S" [about S79E] magnetic, and that if *Hawke* had maintained that course, even if it were on S74E magnetic, she would have gone across *Olympic*'s stern. Instead, he said *Hawke* ported her helm again and came on a parallel course to *Olympic*. Bowyer also admitted that when he was taking the turn around the West Bramble buoy he was not paying any attention to the cruiser because he was certain that he would "get round far ahead of her."

Article 29, which the WSL also claimed was violated by *Hawke*, dealt with negligence.

> ARTICLE 29.
>
> Nothing in these Rules shall exonerate any vessel, or the owner, or master, or crew thereof, from the consequences of any neglect to carry lights or signals, or of any neglect to keep a proper look-out, or of the neglect of any precaution which may be required by the ordinary practice of seamen, or by the special circumstances of the case.

Fig. 5-08 Article 29 from the Regulations for Preventing Collisions at Sea.

Both, counsel for the Admiralty and counsel for the WSL, claimed that Article 29 had been violated by the other side. That comes as no surprise since they both agreed that the collision, which occurred in broad daylight and in relatively fine weather, should never have happened.

---

[1] The bearing lines of the fix were: S88W [252°T] to Egypt Point, S34W [198°T] to the east bank of the River Medina, S31E [133°T] tangent to the east shoreline of the Isle of Wight, and S10E [154°T] to the bathing house on Old Castle Point.

[2] Transcript of the Official Shorthand Writer's Note of the Judgment.

[3] Her starboard engine was running full ahead since 12:35 but the turbine engine was cut out at 12:40 when the port engine was put slow-ahead at the Thorn Knoll buoy.

[4] Captain Smith said that *Olympic*'s full-ahead speed under reduced steam in confined waters was about 20 knots. He also thought that *Olympic* could accelerate from 12 to 20 knots in about 3 or 4 minutes time. *Olympic*'s chief engineer Robert Fleming testified on day 2 of the trial that in his judgment it would take about ¼ of an hour to go from 12 to 20 knots. He also admitted that they never actually measured how long it would take. On day 7 of the trial, Professor of Naval Architecture and Marine Engineering, J. H. Biles, presented data that showed that it would take almost 6 minutes for *Olympic* to accelerate from 15 to 20 knots. Based on our own terminal velocity analysis, we find that it would take about 5 minutes for *Olympic* to accelerate from 12 to 20 knots when carrying a full head of steam at 215 lbs/in^2; the pressure that was actually carried on board the ship that day.

[5] Bowyer placed *Hawke* about 8.8 cables (1,760 yards) NNE magnetic [322°T] of Egypt Point. His point was about 725 yards (3.6 cables) further westward of where Captain Smith had placed her. Bowyer also marked the place of the collision some 160 yards further to the NW magnetic [322°T] of where Captain Smith placed it.

[6] The deviation difference between the steering compass on the bridge and the standard compass on the amidships platform was about 5° when the ship was heading in that direction.

[7] In answer to Question 1498. When asked [Question 1515] why he gave a different answer in cross-examination to the 1 ½ mile answer he originally gave to Question 1431, his response was: "I cannot say exactly."

[8] Transcript of the Official Shorthand Writer's Note of the Judgment.

[9] The circumference of circle is equal to $C = 2\pi R$, where R is the radius taken here at R = 900 ft, and $\pi = 3.14$. One-fourth C is therefore 1,413.7 ft which we rounded to 1,415 ft. *Hawke* had a tactical turning diameter of 588 yards (1,764 ft). The alleged distance apart, 900 ft, happens to be just a little larger than half of *Hawke*'s tactical turning diameter.

[10] If *Hawke* was making 17 knots, it would have taken about 50 seconds (1,415 ft divided by 1,700 ft/min) for the cruiser to strike *Olympic* from the time the swerve started. For this to happen, *Olympic* would have had to cover a distance of about 1,490 ft (900+590) during the time of the swerve, corresponding to almost 18 knots in the final minute before the collision.

[11] If *Hawke*'s bottom had been clean, her full power trial speed with 92 revolutions would have been 18.4 knots. With 3/5 power at 82 revolutions, her speed would have been about 16 ½ knots if she had a clean bottom. *Hawke* had been 11 months out of dock at the time of collision, and it was estimated on 01 November 1911 by Robert Edmond Froude, famous contributor to the Council of the Institution of Naval Architects, that *Hawke*'s speed at 82 revolutions would indeed be reduced from 16.5 knots to about 15.1 knots due to increased resistance caused by fouling on her bottom.

[12] Taking the ratio of the two distances, 1,250 ft/1,415 ft = 0.88 over the same time interval. If *Hawke* was going at 15 knots, then *Olympic* had to be going at just over 13 knots for this scenario to have occurred which is also inconsistent with what was claimed.

Chapter VI

A *HAWKE*'S TALE

Samuel Halpern

The story given by *Hawke*'s officers and bluejackets was very different from that given by *Olympic*'s officers. According to *Hawke*'s officers, *Hawke* was coming up the West Solent Channel on a course N77E magnetic [061° T] carrying 82 revolutions per minute on her engines when *Olympic* was sighted about 2 points off *Hawke*'s port bow and about 3 miles away. She appeared to have just rounded the Calshot Spit after coming out of Southampton Water. At the time, *Hawke* was just south of a line abreast the Gurnard Ledge buoy making a little over 15 knots. According to *Hawke*'s navigation officer, Lt. Reginald Aylen, when *Hawke* passed the Gurnard Ledge buoy at 12:36pm (9 minutes before the collision by *Hawke*'s deck clock), *Olympic* appeared to be about 1 ¾ cables from the North Thorn buoy heading down the Thorn Channel.

As *Hawke* approached Egypt Point, bearing one point before her starboard beam at about 12:40pm, two puffs of steam were seen from *Olympic*'s whistles indicating that she was going to take a turn to port to round the West Bramble buoy. She was reported then about 2/3 the way down between the Thorn Knoll buoy and West Bramble buoy and from 1 to 1 ¼ miles away. As we have seen, this observation agreed with what *Olympic*'s pilot had said as to where *Olympic* was when those two whistle blasts were given. When passing Egypt Point, about 3 ½ cables off, Commander Blunt ordered *Hawke*'s helm be put to port (giving right rudder) to take the turn to starboard to get into the eastern channel. After his ship came around, he gave an order to "steady on the *Edgar*," a cruiser of the same class as *Hawke* that was anchored in Stokes Bay almost in direct line with the Spit Bank Fort that could be seen beyond. This action was to put *Hawke* on a line that would take her close to the three buoys off of Cowes by the Prince Consort Shoal to give *Olympic* as much room as possible to take the channel south of the Ryde Middle. According to *Hawke*'s navigation officer Lt. Aylen, they were originally going to take a course of S85E magnetic [079° T] after rounding Egypt Point to take the channel north of the Ryde Middle, but Commander Blunt changed the course after seeing *Olympic* to put *Hawke* onto S74E magnetic [090° T] to run close to the three buoys.[1]

As both ships were turning, *Olympic* to port and *Hawke* to starboard, the relative bearing line to *Olympic* was drawing aft of *Hawke*'s beam as seen from *Hawke*. According to Commander Blunt, *Olympic* may have steadied on S59E after turning the Bramble after *Hawke* had steadied onto S74E thereby putting them on converging courses of about 15 degrees. When *Olympic* appeared to come out of her turn, her bows were in line with *Hawke*'s stern, and the distance off was estimated to be between 1 and 1 ¼ cables. *Olympic* soon arrived about 100 yards [1/2 cable] abreast of *Hawke* with her bow in line with *Hawke*'s forebridge as *Hawke* was passing within 30 yards [0.15 cables] of the red and white chequered buoy, the middle of the three buoys off the entrance to Cowes. He also said *Olympic* and *Hawke* were then on approximately parallel courses.[2]

Commander Blunt waited until his ship could clear the eastern red conical buoy (the Prince Consort buoy) when he gave the order "port 5, steer for the right hand fort [No Man's Land Fort]" as *Olympic* was seen to be overtaking them and coming somewhat closer. According to Commander Blunt, the alteration of *Hawke*'s course was not much over a point. In his summary statement that he wrote after reaching Portsmouth on 20 September 1911, the day of the collision, Blunt wrote that *"Olympic* passed *Hawke* at about 60 yards [0.30 cables] off." However, on 21 November 1911, day 4 of the court trial that followed, Commander Blunt said that *Olympic* came bridge-to-bridge about ¾ cables abreast of *Hawke* when he gave the order to "steer for the right hand fort" after coming up to the Prince Consort buoy on his starboard hand.

At about the time *Hawke* got the fort ahead of her, her bow began to pay off back to port despite carrying 5° of port helm (right rudder). Commander Blunt then yelled down "What are you doing? Port! Hard-aport!" and ordered "Stop port [engine] full astern starboard [engine]." The quartermaster at the wheel started to turn the wheel over hard but the helm jammed at 15 degrees.[3] Although *Hawke* had 15° of port helm (right rudder) on, *Hawke*'s head continued to veer to port, being pulled toward *Olympic* as if she was under hard-astarboard helm. Seeing this, Blunt quickly yelled down "Full astern both" as he jumped down the ladder and personally worked the port engine telegraph while three people were trying to free the jammed wheel. Despite all efforts, *Hawke* continued her swing to port and struck *Olympic* near her stern after turning about 6 points (about 67°) according to Lt. Aylen. The time of collision taken from the chartroom clock showed 12:45.

According to Lt. Aylen, when *Hawke* was off the western red conical buoy, which she passed at about 30 yards off, *Olympic* was off his port beam and still coming around with her bows in line with *Hawke*'s second funnel.[4] She was then about 300 yards [1 ½ cables] and closing with her head pointed about 1 ½ to 2 points (about 17 to 22 degrees) toward *Hawke*'s course. At the middle red and white checkered buoy, which *Hawke* passed at about 20 yards off according to Aylen, *Olympic* came in line with *Hawke*'s mainmast and was about 70 yards off [0.35 cables] steering what appeared to be a parallel course to *Hawke*. When off the eastern red conical buoy, which *Hawke* passed at about 30 yards off, *Olympic*'s bow was square on to *Hawke*'s and about 50 to 60 yards [0.25 to 0.30 cables] away. Commander Blunt believed he was in line with *Olympic*'s [amidships] compass platform when an uncontrollable swerve to port began, an observation agreed to by *Olympic* eyewitnesses. According to Lt. Geoffery Bashford, *Hawke*'s Officer of the Watch (OOW) at the time, when the "hard-aport" order came down from Commander Blunt, *Hawke*'s forebridge appeared abreast of *Olympic*'s two aftermost funnels.

Commander Blunt said that he believed this was a case of crossing vessels, not overtaking vessels, because *Olympic* was never more than two points abaft his beam. He maintained that *Olympic* came into the channel south of the Ryde Middle on crossing courses.

From the above we can get a good picture of events as related by eyewitnesses on *Hawke*. We also know the distances between the three buoys off of the entrance to Cowes that were referred to, and can therefore calculate the relative times that *Hawke* was off each buoy since it was claimed that she was advancing at a speed of 15 ¼ knots.[5] In addition, we were also told that the collision took place about 3 cables from the Prince Consort buoy by Lt. Aylen and also by *Olympic*'s pilot George Bowyer. They differed only as to what the bearing was from the buoy.[6]

The diagram below (Figure 6-01) shows the positions of *Olympic* and *Hawke* when *Hawke* was abreast each of the three starboard hand buoys, and also at the time of collision as described by *Hawke*'s officers. At a claimed speed of 15 ¼ knots, *Hawke* would have passed the western conical buoy about 1 minute 25 seconds before reaching the Prince Consort buoy (the easternmost of the three buoys), and would have passed the middle red and white chequered buoy about 30 seconds later, or 55 seconds before reaching the Prince Consort buoy. With the claim that the collision took place about 3 cables off the Prince Consort buoy, the easternmost of the three, the time of collision would have taken place about 1 minute 10 seconds after *Hawke* passed the Prince Consort buoy when she had the No Man's Land Fort a little over a point off her starboard bow.

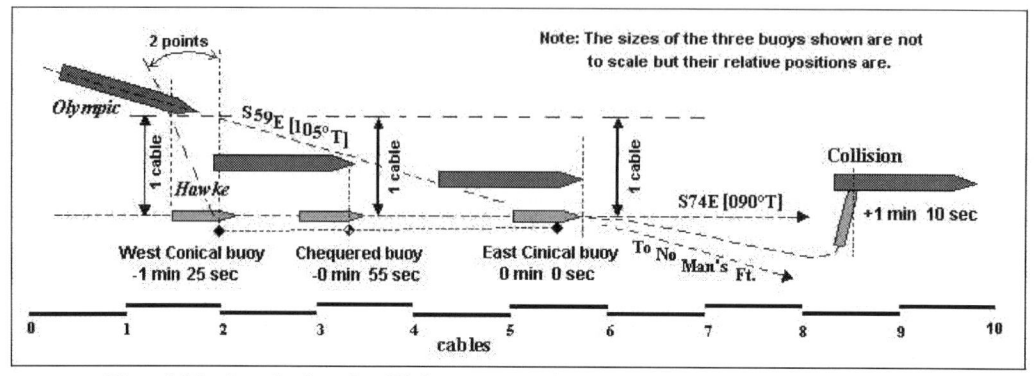

Fig. 6-01 Analysis of collision according to story of *Hawke*'s officers.

As we have seen, both Commander Blunt and Lt. Aylen said that *Olympic* was on a converging course toward *Hawke* after she apparently completed her turn around the Bramble. If *Hawke* had steadied onto S74E as claimed by *Hawke*'s officers, and *Olympic* had steadied onto her course of S59E as claimed by *Olympic*'s officers, the angle of convergence between the two ships would indeed have been 15 degrees. Commander Blunt thought *Olympic* was about 1 to 1 ¼ cables off at the time, while Lt. Aylen thought she was about 1 ½ cables off. Blunt also said that *Olympic* was never more than two points abaft his port beam when she came out of her turn. However, by the time *Hawke* reached the chequered buoy, it was claimed that *Olympic*'s stem was about up to *Hawke*'s forebridge, and according to Blunt and Aylen, the two vessels were running approximately parallel to each other about ½ cable apart as shown above in Figure 6-01.

For this scenario to play out, *Olympic* had to have turned almost 15 degrees to port within about 30 seconds, the time it took *Hawke* to come up to the chequered buoy after passing the west conical buoy. Such a turn by *Olympic* was possible if *Olympic* had not completely steadied onto her prearranged S59E courseline but continued turning to port onto a course that was almost parallel to that of *Hawke*.[7] *Olympic*'s helmsman at the time, Quartermaster Albert Haines, testified that he had the No Man's Land Fort two points on his starboard bow when *Olympic* was steadied onto her course after turning the Bramble. The bearing to that fort would have been only a degree or two on *Olympic*'s starboard bow if *Olympic* had actually steadied onto S59E magnetic as claimed by her officers, not two points on the bow as claimed by Haines.[8]

What could be seen about one point off *Olympic*'s starboard bow, assuming *Olympic* had steadied onto her stated S59E magnetic courseline, is the Puckpool Battery near the town of Ryde on the Isle of Wight. This battery included two 10.4 inch RML guns placed on protected barbette carriages as well as some other ordinance. However, if it really was the No Man's Land Fort that Haines saw about two points on his starboard bow, then *Olympic* had to have been steering a course almost parallel to *Hawke*, a course which would have had the Spitbank Fort ahead of them and the No Man's Land Fort about two points on the starboard bow (Fig. 6-02). Such an action is only likely to have taken place if *Olympic* had swung too far southward when rounding the West Bramble buoy, something that *Hawke*'s officers had claimed she did, and Bowyer wanted to get her back to the middle of the channel south of the Ryde Middle before turning onto her prearranged S59E courseline. If that is what Bowyer did, then that action was not spoken about by any of *Olympic*'s witnesses at the court trial.

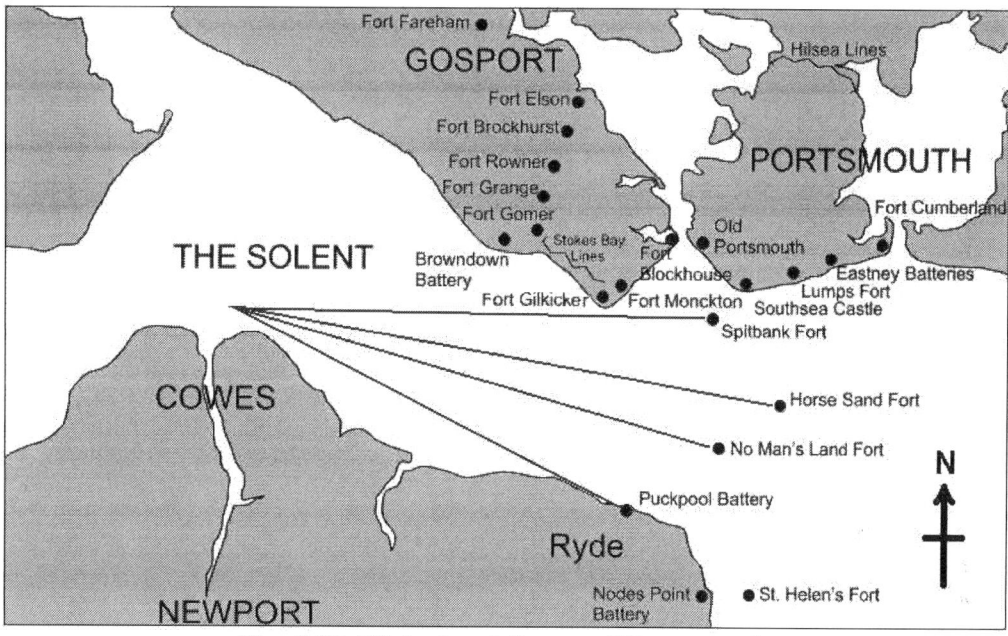

Fig. 6-02 Victorian defenses of Portsmouth.

The evidence from other *Hawke* eyewitnesses also differed greatly from the story given by eyewitnesses for *Olympic*.

Signalman Albert Porter said he came up from lunch at 12:35 and saw *Olympic* nearly abeam 70 to 80 yards [0.35-0.40 cables] off and heard the order given to steady on the *Edgar*. Then 3 to 4 minutes later he heard the order for hard-aport and the report back that the helm was jammed. He also saw the three men trying to free the helm when the order for full speed astern came down. He also said he saw the chequered buoy being passed close by on the starboard side.

AB Alfred Crookham was the lookout on the foremast when he first reported *Olympic* 4 points off his port bow coming out of Southampton Water about 12:30. He continued to watch *Olympic* and saw her turn the West Bramble buoy. He said that she came onto a course which appeared to be parallel to *Hawke*'s about 120 yards [0.6 cables] off his port beam. To him it seemed that they were steaming together for about 5 minutes as *Olympic* gained speed and drew ahead. Then, as he noticed *Olympic*'s aftermost funnel come up on his port beam, *Hawke*'s head "paid off to port very rapidly, more rapidly indeed, I think, than a ship does pay off." He then witnessed the collision. Shortly before this took place, he noticed *Hawke* passing close to two buoys on his starboard hand.

Leading Seaman Henry Yeates came up to take *Hawke*'s wheel at 12:30pm but couldn't remember the course that was given to him. About 5 minutes before the collision he received the order to "Steady on the Edgar." He got 5 degrees of port helm and just about got his ship steadied on the *Edgar* when the quartermaster took the wheel from him by order of Lt. Bashford, the OOW. Yeates then noticed *Olympic* coming upon his port hand from slightly abaft the beam at about 100 yards [½ cable] and overtaking *Hawke*. The next order he heard was "hard-aport" and the QM at the wheel reported the helm jammed. He and Lt. Bashford assisted in trying to get it to free up, but it remained jammed at 15° of port helm when the collision happened. He was also the one to put the starboard telegraph over to full astern when that order was given.

Petty Officer First Class Ernest Hunt relieved the deck at 12:30. Yeates was at the wheel. The course turned over to him was N77½E by standard compass. He first noticed *Olympic* coming out of Southampton Water, but did not notice her again until she was off his port beam at a distance of about 150 yards [about 0.75 cables]. The first order he heard given to Yeates, the helmsman, was "port 15" followed by the order "steady," and noticed the ship steadied on S75E on the steering compass. The next order given was "steady on the *Edgar*," and Yeates seemed to have some difficulty in carrying out that order. It was then that he was told to take the wheel from Yeates and got *Hawke* steadied on the *Edgar*. Later he received an order of "Port 5, steady on the right hand fort [No Man's Land]." Hunt said that his ship answered her helm but he never got his ship to steady on the fort because his ship's head was swinging back [to port] and saw *Olympic* come into view coming across his bow. The next order he heard was "Port! Hard-aport!" He started to put the wheel over hard but it jammed at 15 degrees. AB Yeates and Lt. Bashford then came to help with the wheel but it remained stuck. He was able to free it only after the collision took place when it was put amidships. The last time the helm was altered to starboard was when he steadied on the *Edgar* to stop the swing of the ship to starboard. He also said that he did not notice any oscillation of the steering compass before the collision. It was Hunt who took the time of the collision from the chartroom clock that was behind him.

Lt. Geoffery Bashford took over as OOW at 12:35pm and saw *Olympic* 2 to 3 points off his port bow about 2 miles away with her port side just open to *Hawke*. When Commander Blunt arrived on deck, *Olympic* was about 4 points off his port bow about 1 ½ miles away practically dead-on to *Hawke*. He then saw two puffs of steam from one of *Olympic*'s funnels as she started to round the West Bramble buoy. This was when *Hawke* was about abeam Egypt Point. He heard Blunt give an order to port the helm (the amount he could not recall) and then to steady. He then went down from on top of the chart house to the wheel after hearing Commander Blunt give the order to steady on the *Edgar*. Seeing the helmsman having a bit of difficulty keeping his ship steadied on the *Edgar*, he ordered QM Hunt to take over the wheel. It was about 2 or 3 minutes after they steadied on the *Edgar* that he noticed *Olympic* come into view past his port-side screen about a cable off, and got a glimpse of a red chequered buoy being passed close by their starboard side. A few seconds after seeing *Olympic* come into view he heard Blunt give the order "Port 5, steer for the right hand fort." The next thing he heard was Blunt shouting, "What are doing with your helm? – Port! Hard-aport!" as the helm indicator was showing 5° port. He then said "that the quartermaster started to put the wheel over hard aport, that is from left to right, and at 15 degrees of port helm [seen on the helm indicator] the quartermaster reported the helm jammed, which report I repeated."

As Bashford was helping trying to free the wheel, Commander Blunt called down "Stop port [engine], full speed astern starboard [engine]." Blunt then jumped down the ladder from above and called out "Full speed astern, both!" as *Hawke* continued with a very rapid swing to port and struck *Olympic* on her quarter at about an angle of 5 points [56°] as he was standing by the wheel.

As we have seen, the testimony of witnesses for *Hawke* was somewhat similar in detail regarding the position of both ships after *Olympic* completed her turn around the West Bramble buoy. However, unlike witnesses for *Olympic*, *Hawke* eyewitnesses placed *Olympic* slightly abaft *Hawke*'s beam perhaps a little over a cable off on a converging course to that of *Hawke* which had already completed her turn around Egypt Point onto a line that ran almost parallel to a line of buoys off the entrance to Cowes. Almost dead ahead of *Hawke*, and anchored several miles away in Stokes Bay, was HMS *Edgar* on which *Hawke* steadied. As it turned out, *Hawke* had to wait until she passed the easternmost of the three buoys, the Prince Consort buoy, before she could turn onto a course toward the No Man's Land Fort, the rightmost of three forts that could be seen out of four that were built in the Solent to protect the eastern approaches to Portsmouth.[9] It was while *Hawke* was turning toward that fort under 5° of port helm, attempting to turn to starboard, that she began a violent swerve toward *Olympic* despite carrying port helm (right rudder).

The following chart (Fig. 6-03) shows the courses taken by *Hawke* as claimed by her officers and bluejackets. Also shown are the location of *Hawke* and *Olympic* when *Hawke* was abreast the Gurnard Ledge buoy at 12:36pm, when Egypt Point was one point before *Hawke*'s starboard beam and two puffs of steam were sighted coming from *Olympic*'s whistles at 12:40pm, and when *Hawke* was abreast the west conical buoy which had to be about 12:43pm based on a speed of 15 ¼ knots.[10] Also shown is the fix taken by Lt. Aylen after *Hawke* came to a stop following the collision, and the position where the collision allegedly took place according to Lt. Aylen.[11]

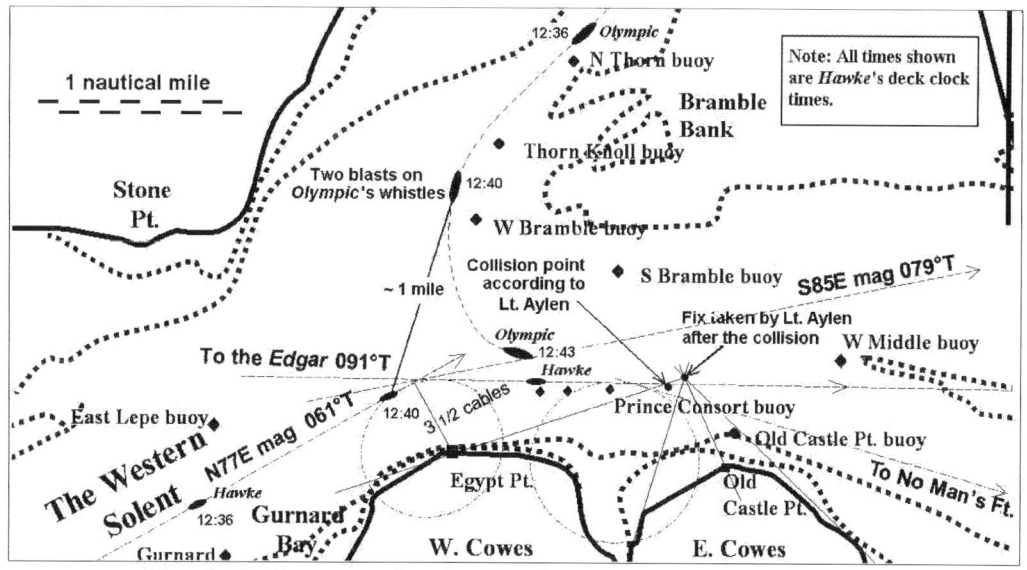

Fig. 6-03 Courses taken by *Hawke* as claimed by her officers.

According to what was logged by *Olympic*'s sixth officer Harold Holehouse, *Olympic* was abeam the Thorn Knoll buoy at 12:40pm and had the West Bramble buoy abeam at 12:42pm. However, *Olympic*'s wheelhouse clock, which incremented by one minute intervals, was running about a minute ahead of *Hawke*'s deck clock, the accepted reason why *Olympic* recorded 12:46 as the time of collision while *Hawke* recorded 12:45 as the time of collision. If it took *Olympic* about two minutes to run the distance between the two buoys, then it would have taken *Olympic* about 80 seconds to go the 2/3 distance down from the Thorn Knoll to the West Bramble thereby reaching the point where she sounded two blasts on her steam whistles about 40 seconds before coming abreast of the West Bramble buoy. The time on *Hawke*'s deck clock would have shown about 20 seconds past 12:40 assuming *Olympic* reached the West Bramble buoy at precisely 12:41 as seen on *Hawke*'s deck clock (12:42 recorded on *Olympic*). The sighting of *Olympic* by *Hawke* two-thirds the distance down from the Thorn Knoll at about 12:40pm when those whistle blasts were sounded is thus confirmed. Given the location of *Hawke* as claimed at that time, with Egypt Point about a point before her starboard beam, *Olympic* would be only 1 to 1 ¼ miles away. By 12:43pm, *Hawke* would have reached the western conical buoy, and about 2 ½ minutes later, between 12:45 and 12:46pm, she would have reached the marked collision point.

Hawke's Engineer Commander George Crichton testified that *Hawke* was making 82 revolutions per minute since noon with her telegraphs showing one-half ahead for the 3/5 power trial.[12] He said that at 12:48 the telegraphs went from ½ ahead to stop, then to full astern. He then felt the impact of the collision about a minute later followed by an order to close all watertight doors. The order to stop engines then followed, and the engines came to a final stop at 12:50. The times recorded for these events were by the engine room clock which was noted as being about 3 minutes ahead of the time kept on the deck clock on the upper bridge.

A copy from *Hawke*'s official logbook (Fig. 6-04) does not give much insight into the collision. The logbook entry from 12pm onward only lists the following in the Remarks column:

P.M.

12-45	Helm jambed. Full speed astern. Struck S.S. *Olympic* on starb. quarter. Collision Stations.
12-50	Stopped. Put Collision Mat over stem.
1-30	Ahead both. Course & Speed as Req. for Harbour.
3-0	Stopped Both. Tug came alongside with Pilot.
3-10	Proceeded up Harbour.
3-50	Stopped both.
4-0	Secured alongside Boat House Jetty.
6-30	Gave usual leave. Steam pumps on Fore Compartments.
8	--------------------0--------------------0
11-30	Hailed Guard Boat. Midnight.

Included on the same page were the bearing lines for the fix taken by Lt. Aylen:

    Position when struck 12-45 pm.
        E. Bank R. Medina   S34W
        Bathing House   S10E
        Egypt Pt.   S88W
        –>|– [tangent line]   S31E

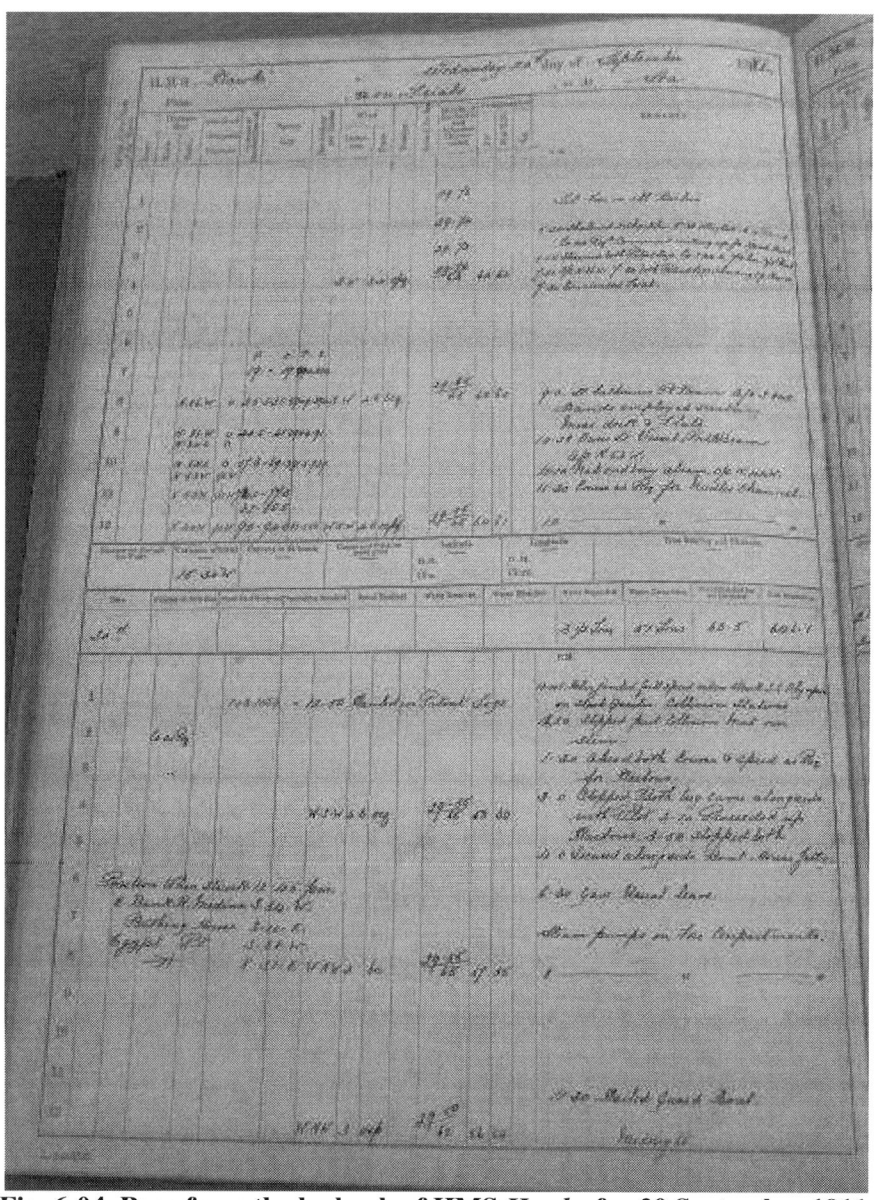

Fig. 6-04 Page from the logbook of HMS *Hawke* for 20 September 1911.

The last bearing written down was for a line tangent to the east shoreline on the Isle of Wight. These four bearings were taken after *Hawke* came to a stop about 5 minutes after the collision, not at 12:45 which was the time *Hawke* struck *Olympic* as put down by Lt. Aylen.

The main thrust of counsel for the Admiralty was that *Olympic* was in violation of Articles 19, 22 and 23 in the Regulations for Preventing Collisions at Sea that were then in effect. The key argument was that *Olympic* was a crossing vessel on a converging course with *Hawke*, having *Hawke* on her starboard side anywhere from 4 degrees on the starboard bow to no more than 2 points abaft the starboard beam after she came out of the turn around the West Bramble buoy. As such, *Olympic* was bound to give way to *Hawke* under these rules and avoid crossing ahead by either slackening speed, stopping or reversing her engines. *Olympic* did none of these, but was accelerating ahead of *Hawke* when the accident happened.

ARTICLE 19.

When two steam vessels are crossing, so as to involve risk of collision, the vessel which has the other on her own starboard side shall keep out of the way of the other.

ARTICLE 22.

Every vessel which is directed by these Rules to keep out of the way of another vessel shall, if the circumstances of the case admit, avoid crossing ahead of the other.

ARTICLE 23.

Every steam vessel which is directed by these Rules to keep out of the way of another vessel shall, on approaching her, if necessary, slacken her speed or stop or reverse.

Fig. 6-05 Articles 19, 22 and 23 from the Regulations for Preventing Collisions at Sea.

Counsel for the Admiralty also claimed that *Olympic* violated Articles 24, 27, 28 and 29 of the rules. As we have seen before, Article 24 is the rule that says that a vessel overtaking another vessel must give way. Yet Commander Blunt testified that *Olympic* was not 2 points abaft *Hawke*'s beam and therefore could not be considered an overtaking vessel according to the rule. However, he did consider *Olympic* a crossing vessel with *Hawke* on her starboard side.

Article 27 has to do with what those in charge of a vessel should take into consideration when deciding to obey or depart from the regulations.

> ARTICLE 27.
>
> In obeying and construing these Rules, due regard shall be had to all dangers of navigation and collision, and to any special circumstances which may render a departure from the above Rules necessary in order to avoid immediate danger.

Fig. 6-06 Article 27 from the Regulations for Preventing Collisions at Sea.

The point of bringing up this rule was to support the claim that the much more massive *Olympic* failed to consider the effects of hydrodynamic interaction between two vessels in a narrow waterway by accelerating past *Hawke*.

Rule 28, as we have seen before, deals with a ship signaling her intentions to another ship by sounding one, two or three blasts on her whistles, depending on the course of action intended. It seems strange that counsel for the Admiralty would claim that *Olympic* was in violation of this rule since multiple eyewitnesses for *Hawke* said they saw the two blasts from *Olympic*'s steam whistle before *Olympic* took the sharp turn to port around the West Bramble buoy. These same witnesses also admitted that *Hawke* never bothered to signal her intentions to *Olympic* before *Hawke* took the turn to starboard around Egypt Point.

Finally, as we have also seen before, Rule 29 dealt with negligence, and each side claimed that this rule was violated by the other side by failure to keep a proper lookout or take proper precautions to prevent a collision.

---

[1] The actual course heading to the *Edgar* when *Hawke* was off the chequered buoy, the middle of the three buoys by the Prince Consort Shoal, was later proved to be S73E magnetic [091° T]. Lt. Aylen said he saw *Hawke* was steadied onto S74E when he looked at the standard compass after they turned Egypt Point, and then heard Commander Blunt give the order to the helmsman to steady on the *Edgar*.

[2] This was at the Admiralty Hearings held in Portsmouth on 22 September 1911, just two days after the accident.

[3] Hard over helm on *Hawke* would have produces 35 degrees of helm.

[4] *Hawke* had two funnels. The second funnel was located about amidships.

[5] The distance of the western conical buoy from the chequered buoy was 1.3 cables, and the distance of the chequered buoy from the eastern Prince Consort buoy was 2.2 cables. The three buoys were on a line that ran 089° T.

[6] Bowyer said the collision took place about 3 cables NE magnetic [029°T] of the buoy, while Lt. Aylen said it took place about 3 cables S87E magnetic [077°T] of the buoy.

[7] From a study of *Olympic*'s turning characteristics, it would take about 17 seconds for *Olympic* to turn 15° degrees in a steady state turn at a speed of 17.5 knots with her helm hard over and all engines at full ahead. That is a turning rate of about 0.9° per second. (Refer to: http://titanic-model.com/articles/Two_Points_in_Thirty_Seven_Seconds/Two%20Points%20in%20Thirty-Seven%20Seconds.pdf)

[8] Haines was questioned about his knowledge of points and degrees. He knew that one point is 11 ¼ degrees and said that the No Man's Land Fort was bearing "about 22 degrees" on his starboard bow. He also said that the ship was steered by degrees, not points, and that the ship was steadied on S64E as seen on the steering compass in front of him. That would also imply that the steering and standard compasses differed by 5 degrees when *Olympic* was heading in that direction, which is quite reasonable.

[9] The three forts that could be seen ahead, from north to south, were: Spitbank Fort, Horse Sand Fort and No Man's Land Fort. The fourth fort that was built, St Helen's Fort, was not visible from where *Hawke* and *Olympic* were at the time.

[10] These times are all by reference to *Hawke*'s deck clock.

[11] As previously noted, it was subsequently found out that the three buoys by the Prince Consort Shoal as marked on the Admiralty charts in use at the time were placed about 1/3 cable south of where the buoys were actually located.

[12] Although the engine order telegraphs were calling for one-half power ahead, the engine room was told that they were to maintain 3/5 power for the trial. The telegraphs did not have a 3/5 indication.

Chapter VII

IN SEARCH OF REALITY

Samuel Halpern

In our independent analysis presented here, we relied heavily on analytical methods to determine as best we can the most likely scenario of what happened that early afternoon of 20 September 1911. We tried to minimize reliance on subjective estimates of distances, ship headings seen from afar or estimates of speeds. Such estimates are always subject to error without reference to some fixed frame of reference. Only through careful testing can estimates prove to be essentially true or shown to be false.

The key to analyzing what really happened between *Hawke* and *Olympic* that Wednesday afternoon is to start with the most probable location of the collision and work the problem backward in time to find out where each vessel was at any given point in time. This then could be used to show us a more realistic picture of what actually took place, and to check that against the various claims that were made at the time. This same technique proved to be most successful in analyzing other collisions such as the one between *Stockholm* and *Andrea Doria* that took place in August 1956.[1]

For the two vessels involved in this particular case, the problem is much easier to work for *Hawke* since her speed was essentially constant at a little over 15 knots up until the last few moments before the collision. By working back from the collision point using the courses she followed, we can show where she was at any particular point in time, and then compare that against the available evidence.

For *Olympic* the problem is little more difficult since her speed varied considerably because of a series of complex engine and helm maneuvers that were used from the time she came out of Southampton Water to when she steadied onto her course after rounding the West Bramble buoy. But we do know approximately where she was at various reported times that were recorded in the scrap log. With the aid of a spreadsheet, and a little trial and error, we can narrow down the times at various reported positions a little more accurately than the times that were put down in the log which were taken off of a clock that incremented only once every minute. At a speed of 15 knots, for example, a 30 second uncertainty in recorded time can amount to a difference of 1 ¼ cables, which is almost an *Olympic* ship length in position. For our work here, this can be significant.

So the first problem is to determine where exactly the collision most likely took place. This was something that neither side could agree upon at the trial before the High Court of Justice in November 1911.

According to what we were told, when *Hawke* struck *Olympic*, the force of the collision spun *Hawke*'s head around "like a top" as she was dragged by the more massive *Olympic* about one-half *Olympic*'s length before the two ships disengaged. Immediately after disengaging from *Olympic*, *Hawke* took on a very noticeable 15° list to starboard before she was able to recover, and continued to turn around as she was backing under engines that were put full astern. When Commander Blunt stopped his engines from reversing, *Hawke* was still carrying some sternway, and backed across *Olympic*'s wake for a distance of about his own ship's length before coming to a stop.

When *Hawke* finally came to a stop, her head was facing about SSW magnetic [187° T] and pointing toward the Coast Guard station on East Cowes. At the Admiralty hearing held in Portsmouth on 22 September 1911, Commander Blunt said that when *Hawke* finally came to rest he had the "Old Castle Point buoy on our port hand, and the wreckage of our figurehead about 60 or 70 yards [0.30 to 0.35 cables] ahead of the ship." The figurehead most likely broke off at the moment *Hawke* struck *Olympic*, and is probably a good indication of where in the westward drifting ebb waters of the channel the two vessels collided.

The place where *Hawke* came to a stop was put down on a chart by Lt. Aylen after taking a fix by standard compass off of four landmarks on the Isle of Wight. The magnetic bearings that established the fix were: S88W [252° T] to Egypt Point, S34W [198° T] to the east bank of the river Medina, S10E [154° T] to the bath house on Old Castle Point, and S31E [133° T] tangent to the eastern shoreline on the Isle of Wight. Aylen claimed that the location of the collision was about 3 cables bearing S87E magnetic [077° T] from the Prince Consort buoy. This collision point was about a cable away to the south and west of the position of the fix that he had taken afterward. (Commander Blunt described the collision point as about an *Olympic*'s length westward and a *Hawke*'s length southward from that fix.) However, it should be noted that the Prince Consort buoy, as well as the two fairway buoys that *Hawke* had passed on her starboard hand shortly before the collision, were erroneously marked about 60 to 70 yards too far south on the Admiralty charts then in use.

Shown below in Figure 7-01 is a scale diagram showing the position of the claimed collision point in relation to the fix that was taken by Lt. Aylen and accepted in the final judgment by the court.

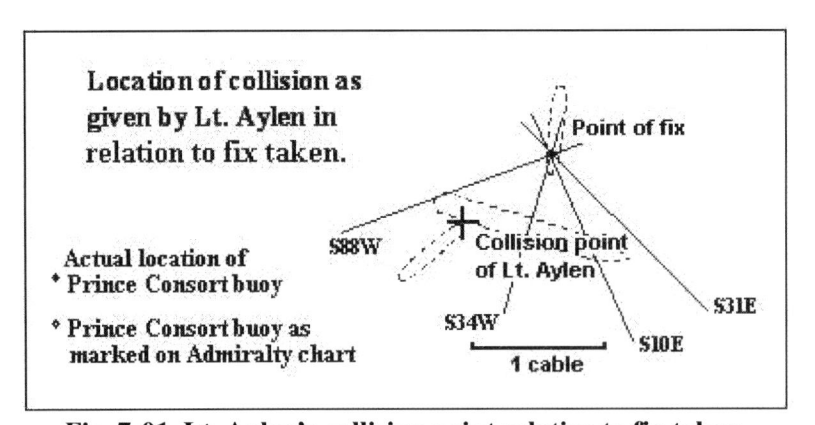

Fig. 7-01 Lt. Aylen's collision point relative to fix taken.

Considering that *Hawke* had been turned around when in contact with *Olympic*, and that her engines were going full astern for about a minute after she separated before the order to stop came,[2] we find that the most likely collision point had to be somewhat *eastward* of the place where *Hawke* finally came to rest.

On Sunday, 11 February 1912, a large piece of wreckage weighing 7 ½ tons was found at a depth of about 80 feet on the bottom of the channel which undoubtedly was part of the lower forefoot of *Hawke*. Damage from *Olympic*'s enormous starboard wing propeller was also visible. According to a report in *Shipping Illustrated* and printed in the US *Naval Institute Proceedings* (Vol. 38, 1912, p. 308):

From private advices it appears that the position of the find was 1200 feet from where the *Hawke* was stated at the trial to have been at the time of collision; that is, 1200 feet more to the eastward and a little more to the north of the channel.

It is most probable that the forefoot of *Hawke* broke off when the two ships separated, which we were told was about one-half *Olympic*'s ship length beyond where they first came into contact. This would therefore place the actual collision point about 700 to 750 feet eastward and a little northward of the collision point put down on the chart by Lt. Aylen, or about ½ cable [100 yards] southeast of the fix that he took from *Hawke*'s bridge 5 minutes after the collision took place.

Another way of getting to the most likely collision point comes from the evidence given by Commander Blunt at the trial regarding the sighting of *Hawke*'s figurehead after *Hawke* came to a stop after backing across *Olympic*'s wake. As previously mentioned, *Hawke*'s figurehead most likely broke off at the moment the two vessels came into contact with each other. It was later sighted floating in the water about 70 yards southward of the point where *Hawke* came to rest. By the time Lt. Aylen took a fix that established where *Hawke* came to rest relative to the land, that figurehead had already drifted westward about 85 yards in the ½ knot ebb tide current that was flowing at the time. Using this information, the description of where in the channel the forefoot of *Hawke* was later seen, as well as the exact location of the fix that was taken by Lt. Aylen, we again find that the most likely point of collision would have been about 100 yards bearing about SE true from Aylen's fix position. This collision point is shown in Figure 7-02 below. It also shows that *Olympic* had to have passed very close to and just south of the location of that subsequent fix taken by Aylen just moments before *Hawke* struck.

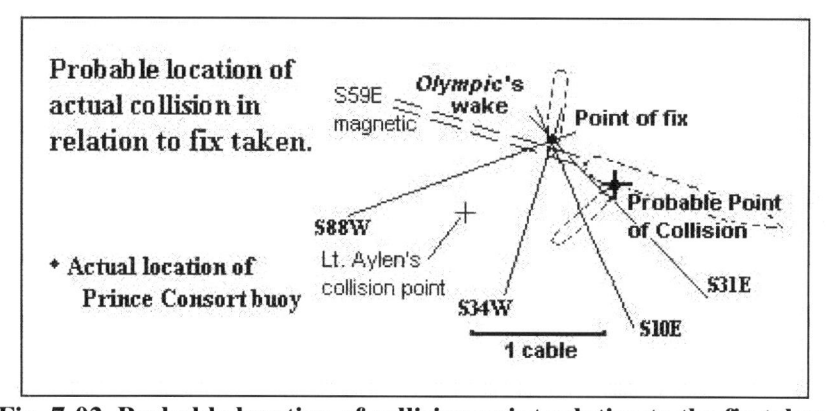

Fig. 7-02 Probable location of collision point relative to the fix taken.

The evidence offered by *Hawke*'s officers as to the distance *Hawke* passed from the three buoys off of the entrance to Cowes on her starboard hand was very difficult to reconcile with the later discovery of wreckage from the collision until 1913 when it was learned that the position of the three buoys indicated on the Admiralty charts in use in 1911 were marked some 60 to 70 yards too far south. As a result, it was later argued by the White Star Line that *Olympic* was indeed more northward and therefore more towards the center of the channel and not as far southward as *Hawke*'s offers had initially claimed.

Unfortunately for *Olympic*, this late realization did not further their claim that *Hawke* was an overtaking vessel that should have kept clear. However, the discovery of the wreckage did suggest that the actual collision happened more eastward and a little more to the north of the collision point put down on the chart by Lt. Aylen and accepted by the High Court in the original judgment that was handed down in December 1911.

Based on a number of eyewitness descriptions, and the above information, an animation sequence was created to show the collision from a few moments before *Hawke* struck to when *Hawke* came to rest a couple of minutes later. A set of selected frames from this sequence is shown in Figure 7-03 for reference.

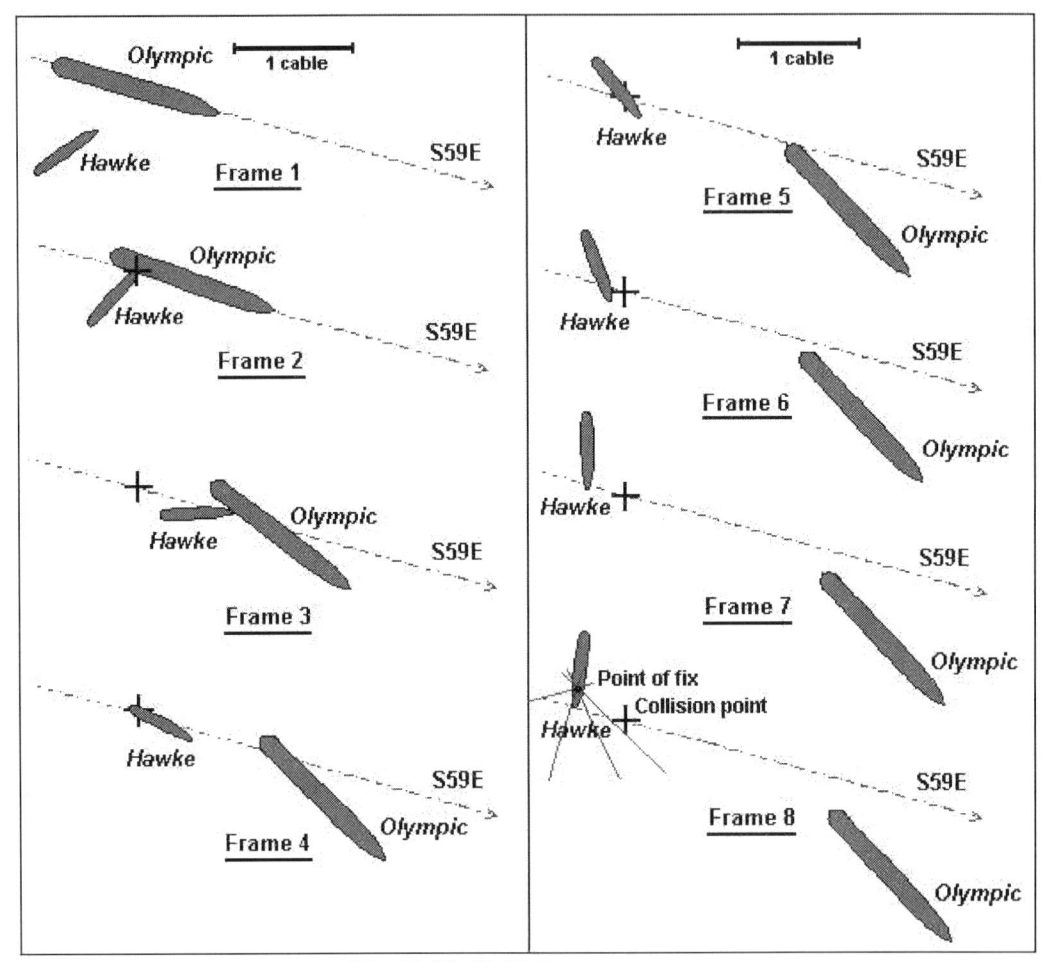

Fig. 7-03 Collision sequence.

To summarize, according to what we were told, *Olympic* steadied on S59E magnetic [105° T] to take the channel south of the Ryde Middle after turning the West Bramble buoy. We were also told that *Hawke* was ordered to steady onto the No Man's Land Fort once she passed a line formed by the Prince Consort buoy and the Old Castle Point buoy which would have put her on a course almost parallel to that of *Olympic*. However, as *Olympic* was rapidly drawing ahead, *Hawke* took an uncontrollable swerve to port as if her helm was put hard-astarboard (left full rudder).

Olympic's helm was ordered to hard-aport (right full rudder) as soon as it was recognized that *Hawke* was going to strike in an attempt to swing her stern away from the oncoming cruiser whose engines it was claimed were put at full speed astern by that time (Frame 1). But all efforts were to no avail as *Hawke* struck the almost seven times more massive ocean liner (Frame 2) despite carrying a jammed wheel that was stuck at 15° port helm (right rudder).

According to Commander Blunt, *Hawke* was dragged about half of *Olympic*'s length as she was spun around before the two ships disengaged (Frames 2-3). Col. Sexton White, a passenger on board *Olympic*, observed *Hawke* recover from a heavy roll to starboard after the two ships separated. He also said *Hawke*'s bow had twisted around to the same direction that *Olympic* was facing having been pulled forward by *Olympic* (Frame 4). According to *Olympic*'s pilot George Bowyers, *Olympic*'s head veered about 3 to 4 points [34° to 45°] to starboard from her channel courseline as a result of the impact from the collision (Frames 3-8). Almost as soon as the two vessels collided, Bowyer ordered *Olympic*'s engines to "stop," and shortly after the ships disengaged he ordered them to "full speed astern" for about a minute to take the way off his stricken ship.

After disengaging from *Olympic*, the damaged *Hawke* continued to swing around to starboard as she was backing under engines that were still running full astern. As *Hawke* was making sternway, she backed across *Olympic*'s wake about her own length before finally coming to a stop pointing about SSW magnetic [187° T] (Frames 4-8).

The next part of the problem is to work out the positions, speeds, and courses that each vessel was on leading up to the collision. The most critical stage to consider is from the time each vessel straightened onto their final courselines up until the moment of collision. The earlier stages of their respective positions, speeds and courses are important only in that they have some bearing on the final positions, speeds, and courses for each vessel.

So what do know with some confidence? The two vessels sighted each other when they were about 3 to 4 miles apart, as *Olympic* was heading down the Thorn Channel passing the North Thorn buoy on a course of S65W magnetic [229° T] and *Hawke* was heading up the West Solent passing the Gurnard Ledge buoy on a course of N77E magnetic [061° T] taking her about half way between the Gurnard Ledge and East Lepe buoys. About 4 minutes later, *Olympic* signaled 2 blasts on her whistles to warn *Hawke* that she was taking the turn around the West Bramble buoy into the East Solent. The distance between the two ship at that time was about 1 to 1 ¼ nautical miles apart, with *Olympic* about 2/3 the distance down between the Thorn Knoll and West Bramble buoys. At that time, *Hawke* was coming up to Egypt Point which was located about 1 point before her starboard beam and about 3 ½ cables off. It was then that Commander Blunt decided to turn his vessel onto a course that would take her close to the line of three buoys off of the entrance to Cowes which would take her into the channel south of the Ryde Middle instead of taking a course S85E magnet [079° T] for the channel north of the Ryde Middle.

The course that *Hawke* steadied onto was S74E magnetic [090° T], and the distance *Hawke* was from Egypt Point after she steadied onto that courseline was also about 3 ½ cables. Soon after *Hawke* came onto that courseline, Commander Blunt ordered his helmsman to steer for the *Edgar*, a cruiser that was anchored in Stokes Bay directly ahead and almost in direct line with the Spitbank Fort that could be seen in the distance beyond. The bearing to *Edgar* when *Hawke* was off the chequered buoy (the second of the three buoys that *Hawke* passed on her starboard hand) was later proved to be S73E magnetic [091° T], confirming what was claimed by *Hawke*'s officers and bluejackets. To give *Olympic* even more room to take the channel south of the Ryde Middle, *Hawke* had to first clear the Prince Consort buoy, the easternmost of the three buoys, coming up on her starboard side. After passing a sightline formed by having the Prince Consort buoy in line with the Old Castle Point buoy beyond, Commander Blunt ordered his helmsman to steer for the "right hand fort," the No Man's Land Fort, which could be seen about 8 miles ahead. The courseline to the No Man's Land Fort from the Prince Consort buoy was about 104.5° true, and this would have put *Hawke* on a course which was essentially parallel to that of *Olympic* when that order was given. The distance that *Hawke* passed the Prince Consort buoy as she was turning for the fort was about 30 yards.

As *Olympic* was coming out of her turn around the West Bramble buoy, the pilot George Bowyer ordered the helmsman to ease the helm as *Olympic* began to come onto S59E magnetic [105° T]. If executed correctly, this course would have put *Olympic* on a line that ran through the center of a long parallelogram formed by four buoys that marked the South Ryde Middle channel. These were the West Ryde Middle buoy over to port and the Old Castle Point buoy over to starboard on the western end of the parallelogram, and the SE Ryde Middle buoy over to port and the Peel Bank buoy over to starboard on the eastern end of the parallelogram. *Olympic* was to maintain that course until she reached the Peel Bank buoy on her starboard hand. If precisely on the center of that courseline, the No Man's Land Fort would be open about a degree or two on her starboard bow. What we do know is that *Olympic* had to have passed just south of, and very close to, the position of the fix taken by Lt. Aylen after *Hawke* came to a stop following the collision. This would have put her within about a cable's length southward of the center of that ideal courseline.

The diagram in Figure 7-04, created by overlaying various details onto a modern day chart of the Solent, shows the course lines taken for both *Olympic* and *Hawke* after completing their respective turns to take the channel south of the Ryde Middle. Shown also on this chart is the location of where the cruiser *Edgar* was anchored (just inside the range of the measured mile buoys off Gilkicker Point) in line with the Spitbank Fort that lay beyond, and also the position of the fix that was taken by *Hawke*'s Lt. Aylen following the collision.

Based on what is known, including how far off each vessel passed various buoys and landmarks in the channel waters, we can chart the courses that both *Hawke* and *Olympic* had taken that fateful September day from a little before the two vessels first sighted each other to the time that they came into contact with each other. This detail is shown in Figure 7-05.

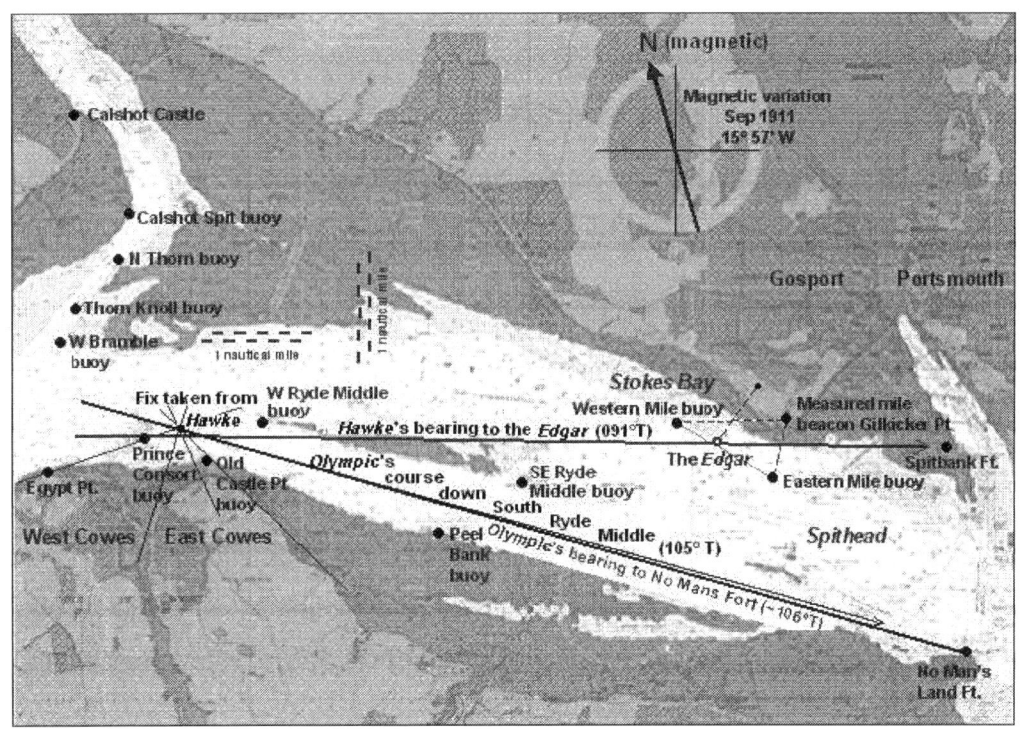

Fig. 7-04 Chart of the East Solent.

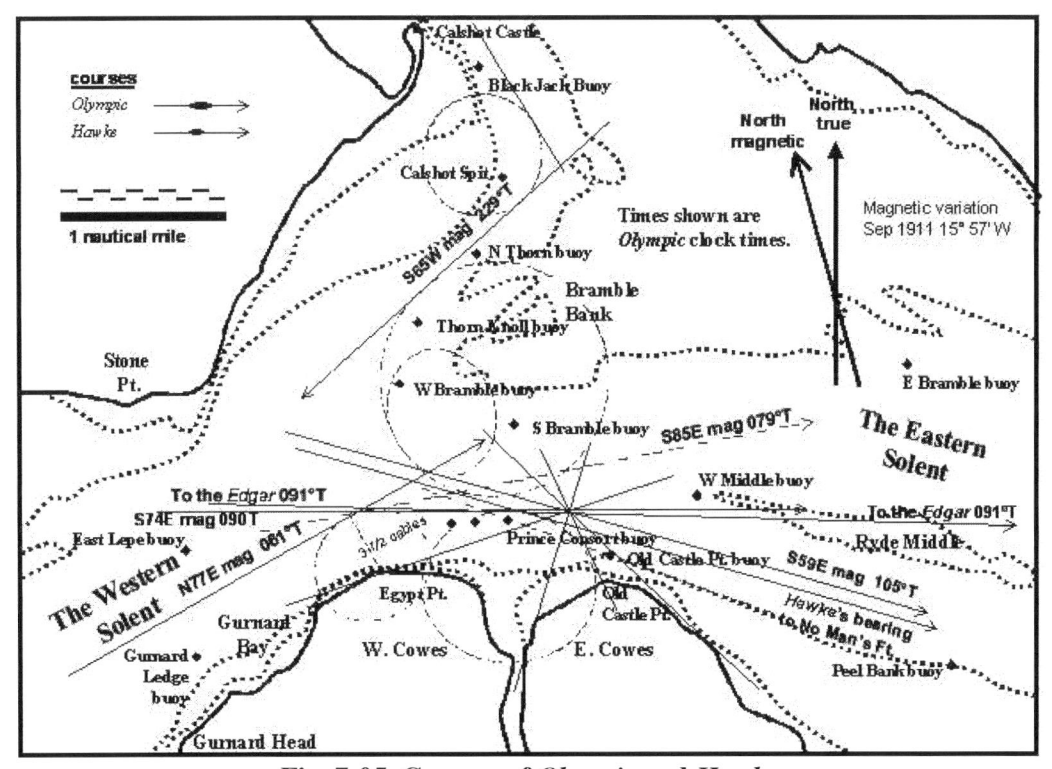

Fig. 7-05 Courses of *Olympic* and *Hawke*.

With the courses of each vessel established, we now have to find where each vessel was at any point in time. For this we will start with *Olympic* since we have a record (shown below) of where she was according to what was recorded in her deck and engine room log books and presented at the High Court trial.

Courses	Time	Events reported for *Olympic*
Calshot Spit to Thorn Knoll S65W	12:27	Half-ahead.
	12:29	Calshot Castle abeam.
	12:30	Blackjack buoy abeam; Slow-ahead.
	12:34	Calshot Spit abeam.
	12:35	Steady on S65W; Full-ahead; Turbine started.
Thorn Knoll to West Bramble Various	12:37	North Thorn buoy abeam.
	12:40	Thorn Knoll buoy abeam; Helm starboard-easy; Slow port, Turbine stopped.
	12:42	West Bramble buoy abeam; Hard-astarboard; Stop port, Half-astern port, Full-astern port.
West Bramble to Peel Buoy S59E	12:43	Steady on S59E; Stop port, Full-ahead port.
	12:44	Turbine started.
	12:46	Struck on starboard quarter by HMS *Hawke*.
	12:47	Stop; Warning bell rung & WTDs closed.
	12:48	Stop engines.
	12:50	Full astern.
	12:51	Stop.

The difficulty that we have with this particular record is that time was taken off of clocks that incremented only once per minute thereby creating an uncertainty of up to 1 minute in the actual time of a reported event. As pointed out before, this can be significant for vessels traveling at speeds of 15 to 20 knots where even 30 seconds can create an error as much as a ship's length or more in position. We also know that for certain events that took place on *Olympic*, such as ordering full ahead on all engines, the order came after the vessel rounded a certain buoy and was being steadied, or about to be steadied, onto a new courseline, not when the vessel actually passed abeam. In addition, there was some finite amount of time taken in opening and closing stop valves and throwing reversing levers when performing certain engine maneuvers. These activities would introduce some additional variances in how long it actually took for the ship to accelerate or decelerate when going from one speed to another. Furthermore, there may have been a 1 minute difference between what was shown on *Olympic*'s wheelhouse clock compared to her engine room clock, a point that came up during the first day of questioning at the High Court trial.

The wheelhouse clock and the engine room clock were controlled from the same Magneta master clock in the chart room. Both clocks where supposed to be checked regularly to ensure that they were keeping the exact same time according to WSL rules that were then in effect (IMM Ship's Rules 305 and 420). However, the workings of the Magneta clock system did not ensure that each slave clock was showing the exact same time as the master clock in the chart room. The mechanism only controlled the moment that each slave clock incremented by one minute of time. In other words, the time changes were synchronized, not necessarily the times shown.

In the deck log, recorded by the sixth officer Harold Holehouse, the time of collision was put down as 12:46, and the stopping of the engines was put down as 12:47. From several eyewitnesses we were told that the order to stop the engines was given by the pilot George Bowyer within seconds of *Hawke* striking, which is entirely understandable. This implies that the recorded strike time of 12:46 had to be within seconds of the wheelhouse clock changing to 12:47. However, in the engine room log, recorded by sixth engineer Duncan Grey, the time of collision and ordering of the stopping of the engines were put down as 12:48, a full minute ahead of the time recorded in the deck log.

Fig. 7-06 Magneta marine master clock.

In examining the events timeline, we have made use of the power of a spreadsheet to determine the average speed of *Olympic* between passing certain positions by dividing the measured distance between those positions along the route traveled by the difference between the specific times attributed for being at those positions. The results obtained were then looked at to see if the average speeds made sense when compared to what we were told about engine and helm maneuvers that were carried out, and the effect that they would have on the speed of the ship.

From the engine room log, we were told that at 12:27 an order for half-ahead was given. This was maintained until the order was given to put the engines at slow-ahead when the ship passed the Blackjack buoy at 12:30. From a previous study of speed as a function of revolutions, we know that *Olympic* would make about 15.5 knots at half-ahead carrying about 50 revolutions per minute on her reciprocating engines with the central turbine engine still connected.[3] In the spreadsheet analysis, shown in the following table, we obtained an average speed of 15.7 knots for the run between Calshot Castle and the Blackjack buoy, a distance of 3.5 cables, with Calshot Castle abeam taken at 12:29:00 and the Blackjack buoy abeam taken at 12:30:20. These two events were recorded in the log book as 12:29 and 12:30, respectively.

Once past the Blackjack buoy, *Olympic*'s engines would be running at slow-ahead carrying about 30 revolutions per minute with the turbine engine disengaged. At slow-ahead, the expected speed of *Olympic* would drop to about 9 knots.

Location	Distance from previous mark (cables)	Distance from collision (cables)	Assigned time at location (hh:mm:ss)	Time from collision (h:mm:ss)	Ave. speed from previous location (knots)
Calshot Castle	n/a	43.6	12:29:00	0:18:00	n/a
Blackjack buoy *	3.5	40.1	12:30:20	0:16:40	15.7
Steady on S65W **	9.0	31.1	12:35:50	0:11:10	9.8
North Thorn buoy	5.0	26.1	12:37:55	0:09:05	14.4
Thorn Knoll buoy *	5.7	20.4	12:39:45	0:07:15	18.7
2 blasts on whistles	3.6	16.8	12:41:00	0:06:00	17.3
West Bramble buoy	2.3	14.5	12:41:50	0:05:10	16.6
Steady on S59E **	4.9	9.6	12:43:50	0:03:10	14.7
Collision	9.6	0.0	12:47:00	0:00:00	18.2

Timeline for *Olympic*

* Turbine taken off line.   ** Turbine connected on line.

The next event listed is after the ship had rounded Calshot Spit when all engines were ordered to full-ahead and the turbine engine connected back up as the ship was being steadied onto S65W magnetic [229° T]. The time the turbine was connected back up was recorded as 12:35. We list this as happening at 12:35:50 thereby giving an average speed between the Blackjack buoy to this location of 9.8 knots, which seems quite reasonable considering that the engines were ordered to slow-ahead when passing the Blackjack buoy and were further maneuvered along with the helm to take the sharp turn around Calshot Spit into the Thorn Channel.

We next list *Olympic* off the North Thorn buoy at 12:37:55 which gives an average speed from when her engines were put to full-ahead to her reaching the North Thorn buoy of 14.4 knots. During this time the ship was accelerating to her full-ahead speed for restricted waters which we were told was about 20 knots. The scrap log entry for when the ship passed the North Thorn buoy was 12:37.

The next reported event was when *Olympic* had the Thorn Knoll buoy abeam. The scrap log listed that as happening at 12:40. As the ship approached the Thorn Knoll buoy, Bowyer ordered "starboard easy" on the helm and ordered the port engine to slow-ahead to take the ship down to the West Bramble. At the same time the turbine engine was disconnected. We have assigned a time of 12:39:45 for the start of those events. Using that specific time, we derived an average speed of 18.7 knots between the North Thorn and Thorn Knoll buoys, which is approaching her full-ahead speed for restricted waters considering the engines were ordered to full-ahead almost 4 minutes earlier after coming out of the turn rounding Calshot Spit.

The next event listed is when Bowyer ordered that two blasts be signaled on *Olympic*'s whistles to inform *Hawke* that *Olympic* was turning to port to take the turn around the West Bramble buoy into the east Solent. This came when *Olympic* was about 2/3 the distance down from Thorn Knoll to West Bramble. We have assigned a time of 12:41:00 for this event.

The next event listed is when Bowyer ordered *Olympic*'s helm be put hard-astarboard and the port engine stopped. This was soon followed by an order to put the port engine to half astern, and then to full astern as the ship was in the process of rounding the West Bramble buoy. For this we assigned a start time of 12:41:50 which results in an average speed of about 17 knots between Thorn Knoll and West Bramble. The scrap log listed those maneuvers at the West Bramble buoy as happening at 12:42.

Prior to reaching the West Bramble buoy, *Olympic* was carrying full-ahead on her starboard engine and slow-ahead on her port engine. This explains why her average speed would drop between the Thorn Knoll and the West Bramble compared to what it was between the North Thorn and the Thorn Knoll. It was estimated by *Olympic*'s pilot George Bowyer that the ship was going at a speed of 15 to 16 knots coming up to the West Bramble buoy, while Captain Smith estimated that she was going at a speed of about 17.5 knots as she approached the buoy. Therefore, a derived average speed of 17.3 knots between Thorn Knoll and when those two whistle blasts were sounded seems quite reasonable, as does a derived average speed of 16.6 knots between the point of the whistle blasts and the start of those maneuvers at the West Bramble buoy.

The next event listed is when *Olympic* was being steadied onto her predetermined courseline of S59E magnetic [105° T] having rounded the West Bramble buoy. For this we assigned a time of 12:43:50. It was about this time that the order was given to stop the port engine and put it to full ahead. The time put down in the scrap log for when the turbine engine was connected back on line was 12:44.

The last event listed is when *Olympic* was struck by *Hawke* and the order given to stop all engines and close the watertight doors. We assigned a time of 12:47:00 to this event giving us an average speed of 18.2 knots from the time the she was steadied onto her S59E magnetic courseline to the time when she was struck.[4] The time put down in the deck log for when *Olympic* was struck by *Hawke* was 12:46; the time put down in the deck log for stopping the engines and closing the watertight doors was 12:47. Those two events came within seconds of each other.

Although we obviously don't really know the actual precise times of these events, the above spreadsheet values give explainable results that seem to match well with the available evidence. We know that the recorded times put down in the scrap log were only to the nearest minute that a clock had last incremented, and that multiple events, such as the stopping of an engine, then putting it to half-astern and then to full-astern, were all put down as if they happening at the same instant of time. As pointed out during the trial, these recorded times could easily have been off by up to a minute, which would produce erroneous results if taken as precise values.

With times and positions established for *Olympic*, we can turn our attention to *Hawke*. For this we make use of the fact that the speed of *Hawke* was maintained at just over 15 knots up until she started to veer toward *Olympic*. It was then that orders were given to stop and reverse her engines in an unsuccessful attempt to avoid an impending collision. We were told that during her full power trial, *Hawke* averaged about 17 knots with 92 revolutions per minute on her engines, and during the 3/5 power trial that followed, she carried 82 revolutions per minute on her engines. Commander Blunt believed *Hawke* was making about 15 ¼ knots during her 3/5 power trial. Taking the ratio of her engine revolutions, we get an average speed of 15.15 knots for the 3/5 power trial assuming *Hawke* averaged precisely 17.0 knots during the full power trial. Therefore, 15 ¼ knots appears to be a justifiable speed to use for *Hawke* in our spreadsheet to derive where *Hawke* was along her courselines as a function of time.[5]

The following table shows the distances of *Hawke* from the collision point for the same instances of time that we used for *Olympic*.

Timeline for *Hawke*				
Event	Assigned time at location (hh:mm:ss)	Time from collision (h:mm:ss)	Distance from collision (cables)	Distance to next time point (cables)
Olympic off Calshot Spit	12:35:50	0:11:10	28.4	5.3
Olympic off North Thorn	12:37:55	0:09:05	23.1	4.7
Olympic off Thorn Knoll	12:39:45	0:07:15	18.4	3.2
2 puffs of steam from *Olympic*	12:41:00	0:06:00	15.2	2.1
Olympic turning W Bramble	12:41:50	0:05:10	13.1	5.1
Olympic steadied onto S59E	12:43:50	0:03:10	8.0	8.0
Collision with *Olympic*	12:47:00	0:00:00	0.0	0.0

Having derived distances from the collision point for each ship, we can now show where each ship was on their respective courses at the times listed. This is shown in the chart below (Fig. 7-07) starting from when *Olympic* was passing the Blackjack buoy up until the time of the collision.

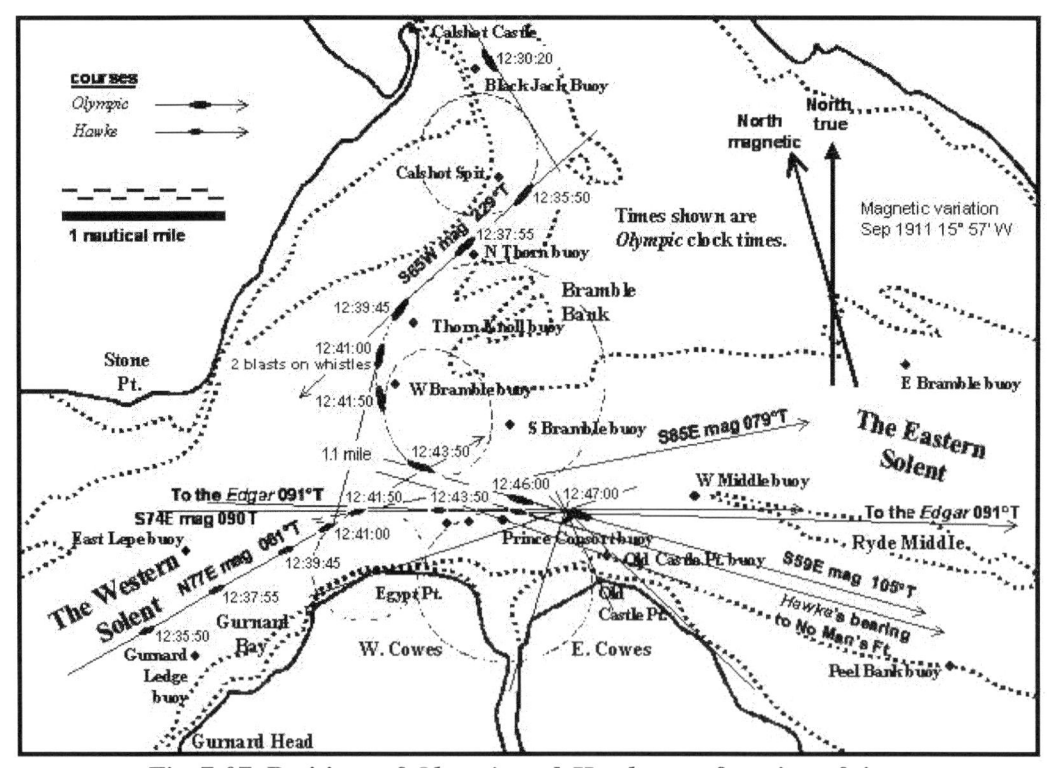

Fig. 7-07 Positions of *Olympic* and *Hawke* as a function of time.

As essentially agreed to by both sides, both vessels gained sight of each other when *Olympic* was between the Calshot Spit and the North Thorn buoys coming down the Thorn Channel, and *Hawke* was passing between the East Lepe and Gurnard Ledge buoys off Gurnard Bay. The distance between the vessels was about 3 nautical miles, and the time would be about 12:37 on *Olympic*. At this time, *Olympic* was heading down on a course of S65W magnetic [229° T], and *Hawke* was heading up on a course of N77E magnetic [061° T].

Of most interest to us is the last 7 minutes and 15 seconds in this timeline before the two ships came together. The diagram below (Figure 7-08) shows a close up of the chart beginning at 12:39:45 when *Olympic* was off the Thorn Knoll buoy, and *Hawke* had Egypt Point about 6 cables broad off her starboard bow. The other events shown include the time when *Olympic* sounded two blasts on her steam whistles indicating the she was going to take the turn around the West Bramble buoy (12:41:00), the start of *Olympic*'s helm and engine maneuvers to sharpen the turn around the West Bramble (12:41:50), the time *Olympic* steadied onto her S59E [105° T] courseline (12:43:50), the situation one minute before the collision (12:46:00) when the two vessels were running almost parallel to each other with the No Man's Land Fort seen ahead of them, and the moment when *Hawke* struck and *Olympic*'s engines were ordered to stop (12:47:00).

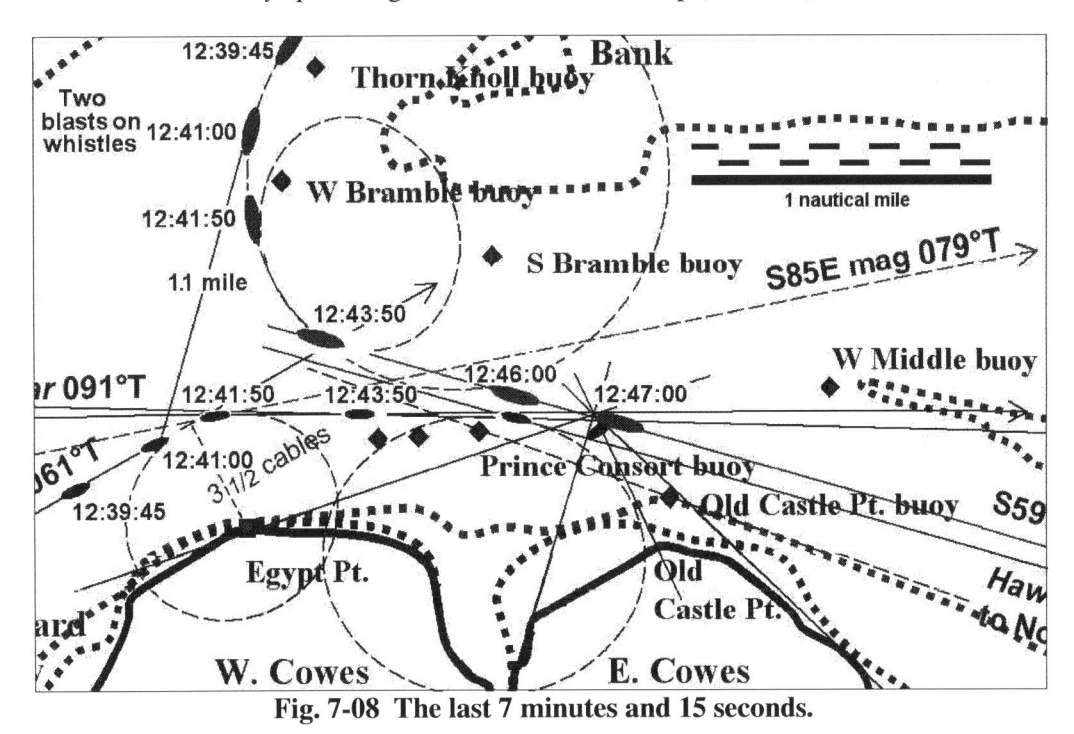

Fig. 7-08 The last 7 minutes and 15 seconds.

As we can see from the diagram in Figure 7-08, when two blasts were sounded from *Olympic*'s whistles, *Olympic* was about 2/3 the distance down from Thorn Knoll to West Bramble, and *Hawke* had Egypt Point a little over a point before her starboard beam about 3 ½ cables off (12:41:00). The distance between the two vessels measures about 1.1 nautical miles on the chart, with *Olympic* starting to open her starboard side to *Hawke* and bearing about 4 points off *Hawke*'s port bow.

About a minute later, *Olympic* would have been past the West Bramble buoy and *Hawke* would be turning to starboard under 15° of port helm (right rudder) to take a courseline (S74E magnetic) that would approximately parallel the three buoys off the entrance to Cowes. If not for *Olympic* being there, *Hawke* would have straightened onto S85E magnetic [079° T] to take the channel north of the Ryde Middle toward Spithead.

From our spreadsheet results, *Olympic* would be averaging about 16 ½ knots as she approached the West Bramble buoy under easy starboard helm (left rudder) with full-ahead on her starboard engine and slow-ahead on her port engine. *Hawke* was averaging about 15 ¼ knots all along. *Olympic*'s pilot, George Bowyer, took notice of the course that *Hawke* was on when he signaled *Hawke* that *Olympic* was going to take the turn around the West Bramble buoy. He estimated that *Hawke* was coming up the Solent on "East by North ¼ North" which is N76E magnetic. (*Hawke* was actually coming up on N77E magnetic, an insignificant difference of only 1 degree.) He also had to know that if *Hawke* did not change her course, she would be crossing his path from *Olympic*'s starboard side. Under the rules of the road, *Olympic* was required to give way to *Hawke* even at that time. This should all be obvious from the expanded chart view shown in Figure 7-08.

So what went wrong? Why did Bowyer continue to take *Olympic* around the buoy the way he did without taking specific action to avoid crossing ahead of *Hawke*?

For one thing, Bowyer said that when he signaled those two blasts on *Olympic*'s whistles, *Hawke* was down by Gurnard Bay about 1 ½ miles distant. This does not agree with what *Olympic*'s second officer, Robert Hume, finally said under cross-examination or what those on *Hawke* said who put the distance closer to about one mile when those two blasts were sounded. This may have been a case of Bowyer simply overestimating the distance between the two vessels at the time it happened, or inflating the distance at the time of the trial to match their side of the story as to what happened afterward. If *Hawke* was really 1 ½ miles away at that time, it would imply that she was about 20 cables from the collision point instead of about 15 cables away at the time the two blasts were sounded. More importantly, it implies that *Hawke* would have to have averaged over 20 knots to reach the point of collision, which was not at all possible.

Bowyer also said that he believed that *Olympic* would get around the West Bramble far ahead of *Hawke* and he therefore did not pay any attention to her after those whistle blasts were sounded. At the time, *Olympic* was doing about 17 knots and *Hawke* was doing a little over 15 knots. Furthermore, *Olympic* would have to slow down even more while taking the turn around the buoy to get onto her desired courseline, something Bowyer also knew in advance. Yet, from what we see in the details above, if *Hawke* would have held to her N77E courseline instead of turning to round Egypt Point, the two vessels would likely have come together at the position where *Olympic* had steadied onto her S59E courseline about 3 minutes later. Under the rules of the road, *Hawke* was under no obligation to change her course or to slow down. *Olympic*, however, was. Either Bowyer seriously misjudged the situation, or assumed that *Hawke* would be the vessel that would take action and fall under his stern after he signaled his intention to take *Olympic* around the buoy into the East Solent.

At the time *Olympic* was still being maneuvered around the West Bramble buoy, *Hawke* was coming onto her S74E courseline to parallel the three buoys off the entrance to Cowes. Soon Commander Blunt ordered the helmsman to "steer for the *Edgar*" as *Hawke* approached the westernmost of those three buoys. By the time *Olympic* had steadied onto her S59E courseline and all her engines put at full-ahead again, *Hawke* was abreast the west conical buoy. As seen from *Hawke*, *Olympic*'s stem would be less than 2 points abaft her port beam on a converging course of about 15 degrees to that of *Hawke*. This is exactly the situation that was described by Commander Blunt and Lt. Aylen except for the distance that the two ships were apart. Commander Blunt said *Olympic* was about 1 to 1 ¼ cables away from *Hawke*, while Lt. Aylen thought she was about 1 ½ cables away. What we show is a distance of about 2 ¼ cables from *Hawke*'s bridge to *Olympic*'s stem at that time.[6] According to *Olympic*'s officers, *Hawke* supposedly was 2 to 3 points off *Olympic*'s starboard quarter and ¼ mile aft when *Olympic* steadied onto her S59E courseline, a situation that simply does not hold up to analysis.

About 30 seconds after passing the west conical buoy *Hawke* had the chequered buoy abeam. *Olympic* was then accelerating once again toward her full-ahead speed for channel waters, and the distance between the two vessels was closing steadily. About 30 seconds after passing the chequered buoy, Commander Blunt was able to see the Old Castle Point buoy directly in line beyond the Prince Consort buoy that was coming up rapidly on his starboard side. It was then that Blunt gave an order to his helmsman "port 5, steady on the right hand fort" which could be seen about 15° off his starboard bow. The intent of Blunt's order was to put *Hawke* on a course that would parallel that of *Olympic*. At this point *Hawke*'s head started to swing slowly to starboard as she passed about 30 yards off the Prince Consort buoy. Commander Blunt estimated he was then only about ¾ of a cable away from *Olympic*. We show the distance at about 1 cable.

At one minute before impact, the two vessels were about bridge-to-bridge with *Olympic* drawing ahead very fast. By this time *Hawke*'s head had turned only about 10 degrees to starboard under the 5° of port helm (right rudder) that had been applied. The angle of convergence between the two vessels was reduced from 15 to about 5 degrees. However, it was about this time that an unexpected hydrodynamic interaction began to take place between the two vessels which stopped *Hawke* from turning to starboard and soon caused her to turn back toward *Olympic*.

The diagram in Figure 7-09 shows the situation we obtained from 3 minutes before collision (-3m 00s), when *Hawke* was abreast the west conical buoy and *Olympic* had steadied onto her S59E courseline, to 1 minute before collision (-1m 00s), when an adverse hydrodynamic interaction between the two vessels began to take effect. During those 2 minutes of time, it is estimated that *Olympic* would have averaged about 18 ½ knots while *Hawke* was maintaining about 15 ¼ knots.

As soon as Commander Blunt noticed that his ship began to pay off back towards the massive ocean liner that was steaming past on his port hand, he yelled down, "What are you doing? Port, port, hard-aport!" QM Hunt never quite got the No Man's Land Fort directly ahead. When Blunt's hard-aport order came down to him, *Hawke* had already swung back to within 6 degrees of her previous courseline toward HMS *Edgar*, and *Olympic* was now only about ½ cable away on his port side. As soon as QM Hunt heard Commander Blunt's order, he quickly spun the wheel hard to his right when it suddenly jammed at 15° of port helm.[7]

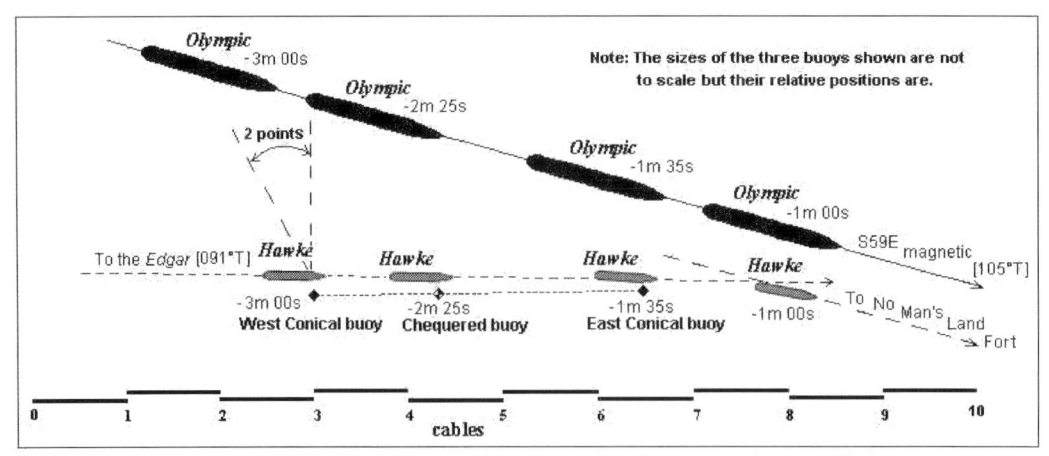

Fig. 7-09 Developing situation from 3 minutes before collision to 1 minute before collision.

As *Hawke* was being unexplainably drawn toward *Olympic*, Captain Smith called out to his pilot George Bowyer, "I do not believe he will go under our stern Bowyer." Bowyer then told Smith, "If she is going to strike let me know in time to put our helm hard-aport." Smith did not reply immediately, and a few seconds later Bowyer asked, "Is she going to strike us or not, sir?" Smith then said, "Yes Bowyer, she is going to strike us in the stern." Immediately, Bowyer sang out, "Hard-aport!" and helmsman Albert Haines just managed to get *Olympic*'s wheel over hard to his right when *Hawke* struck.

The relative positions of the two vessels from 1 minute before impact (-60s) to the moment of impact (00s) in 15 second increments are shown in Figure 7-10. This detailed sequence was created in part from turning circle data for *Hawke* that was presented by Portsmouth's dockyard constructor E. J. Maginnis during the High Court trial.[8] The speed of *Hawke* was taken at 15 ¼ knots, and that of *Olympic* works out to an average of 19 ¾ knots over that last minute of time.[9]

The sequence shows the two vessels starting about bridge-to-bridge and a little more than 3/4 cable apart at 1 minute (t = -60s) before collision. *Olympic* was steady on her S59E magnetic [105° T] courseline taking her south of the Ryde Middle with the No Man's Land Fort seen ahead about 1 degree on her starboard bow at that time. At the same time *Hawke* was almost on a parallel course to *Olympic*, pointing only about 5° toward the massive ocean liner.

Despite carrying 5° of port helm (right rudder), *Hawke*'s head did not continue to turn to starboard. Instead, *Hawke* started to turn back toward *Olympic*. At 30 seconds before impact (t = -30s) *Hawke* was facing about 10 degrees toward *Olympic* with her bridge now in line with *Olympic*'s amidships point. It was at this point in time when those on both vessels fully realized that something was terribly wrong. The remaining sequence shows *Hawke* in an uncontrolled swing toward *Olympic*. At the end of the sequence (t = 00s), *Hawke* strikes *Olympic* almost 90 feet ahead of *Olympic*'s stern. At the time of impact, *Olympic*'s stern was swinging away from *Hawke* under hard-aport helm (40° of right full rudder) that was called for with just enough time to get *Olympic*'s helm hard over.

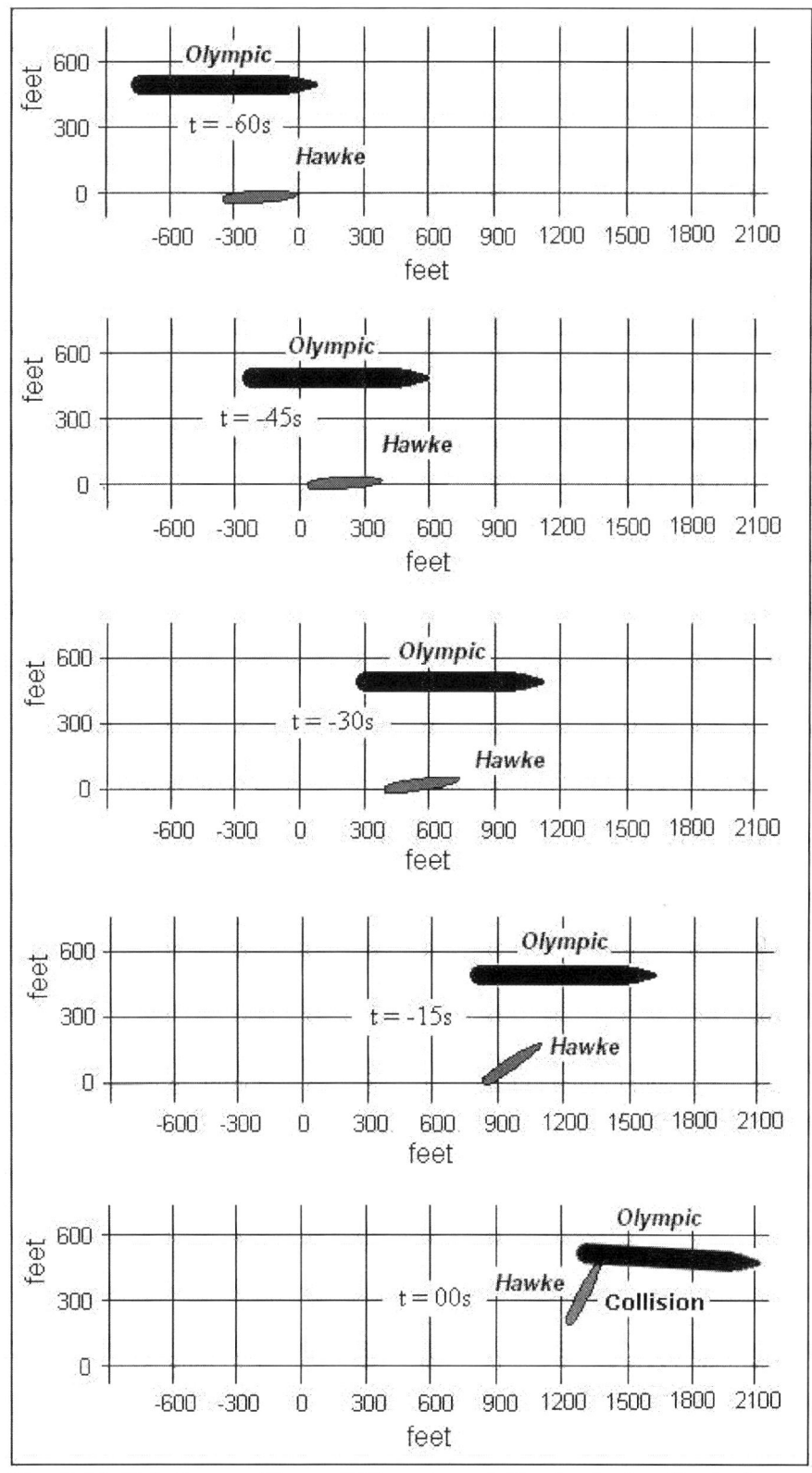

Fig. 7-10 Relative positions of *Olympic* and *Hawke* during final minute.

Based on the damage seen, it was estimated that *Hawke* struck *Olympic* at an angle between about 62 and 79 degrees, depending on the amount of heel that was developed on *Hawke* just prior to the collision.[10] According to *Hawke*'s Lt. Aylen, the strike angle appeared to him to be about 6 points (67.5°), which is what we show in Figure 7-10 and in the scaled diagram in Figure 7-11 below. When the two vessels finally parted, the separation angle was estimate to be about 35 degrees.

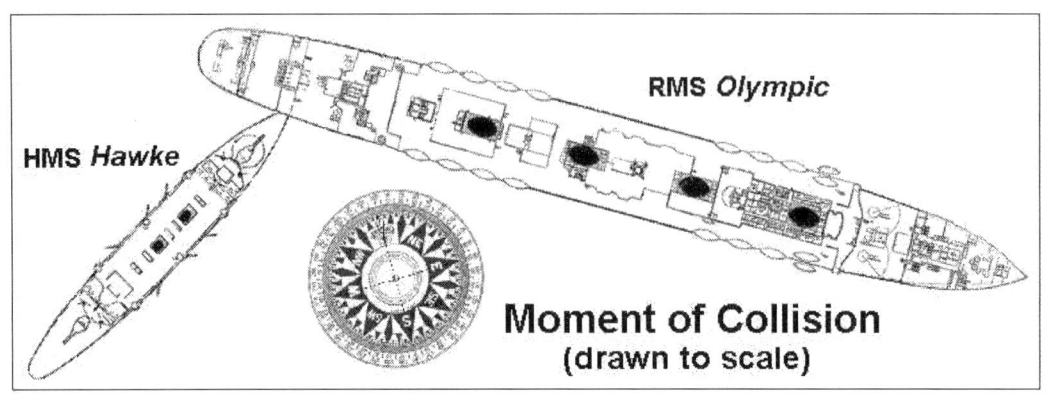

Fig. 7-11 Moment of Collision. *Hawke* strikes *Olympic* at an angle of about 67°.

---

[1] Refer to the article by Samuel Halpern, "Lights to Port – Lights to Starboard," http://www.titanicology.com/AndreaDoria/Stockholm-Andrea_Doria_Collision_Analysis.pdf.

[2] *Hawke*'s engineering commander George Crichton testified that the collision was felt about a minute after the order "Stop-Full Astern" was given. The engine room log showed that that particular order came at 12:48 on the engine room clock, and that the final "Stop" order came two minutes later at 12:50 on the engine room clock. It was also noted that *Hawke*'s engine room clock was 3 minutes ahead of the clock on *Hawke*'s bridge.

[3] The turbine engine, which could only run ahead, was connected up for speeds of half-ahead (about 50 revolutions per minute) or greater on both reciprocating engines. Otherwise, the turbine engine was taken off line by simply throwing a lever which resulted in exhaust steam from the reciprocating engines being redirected from the input to the turbine to the input of the ship's two main condensers. Refer to the on-line article by Samuel Halpern, "Speed and Revolutions," http://www.titanicology.com/Titanica/SpeedAndRevolutions.htm.

[4] Although denied by her engineers, it is entirely possible that *Olympic* was accelerating to a speed greater than her reduced full-ahead speed for restricted waters of 20 knots if her stop valve had been opened up more than the usual number of turns after coming out of the turn around the West Bramble buoy. It was learned during the testimony of Senior 2nd Engineer J. H. Therle that *Olympic* was carrying a full head of steam at 215 lbs per sq. in. since leaving the dock at Southampton. That was enough to drive her at a full-ahead speed of 22 ½ knots when at sea.

[5] The difference between 15.15 and 15.25 knots over an 11 minute period amounts to an insignificant 111 feet out of a total travel distance of nearly 17,000 feet.

[6] If it was true that *Olympic* was about a cable length closer to *Hawke* as claimed by Blunt and Aylen, then *Olympic* would have gone further south of the West Bramble buoy than what we show, and Bowyer would then have to continue with his turn to put *Olympic* on a course to get her more to the center of the channel before steadying on his prearranged S59E courseline. In that case, the No Man's Land Fort would have been about 2 points on *Olympic*'s starboard bow as QM Haines described.

[7] Hard-aport would have produced 35° of right rudder on *Hawke* if the helm had not jammed.

[8] The data showed a tactical diameter for *Hawke* of 588 yards (1754 feet) at 15 knots under full helm.

[9] A speed of 19 ¾ knots is actually very consistent with *Olympic* averaging about 66 revolutions per minute (rpm) on her reciprocating engines during the last minute before the collision. Captain Smith and Chief Engineer Fleming stated at the High Court trial that *Olympic* would make 20 knots carrying 75 rpm in restricted waters. That is not correct. At 75 rpm, *Olympic* would be making almost 22 knots. We know this from actual *Olympic* sea-trial data that was presented by Harland & Wolff naval architect Edward Wilding at the British Inquiry into the loss of *Titanic* where he offered evidence that at 60 rpm *Olympic* made about 18 knots, and at 74 rpm she made about 21 ½ knots (BI 25292-25295).

[10] Evidence was given by consulting naval architects Harry Roscoe and John D. Young at the High Court trial.

Chapter VIII

DAMAGES AND REPAIRS

Mark Chirnside and Samuel Halpern

At the moment of collision, *Hawke* penetrated about 8 feet into *Olympic* producing a large triangular hole from above D deck to 15 feet below. F and G decks were penetrated by *Hawke*'s ram, and there was broken plating from D deck down to G deck. The center of the two large holes produced was 86 feet ahead of *Olympic*'s stern post. Penetration was at frame 113 at the forward corner of the top hole. The starboard side of *Olympic* was scored aft of the hole for about 38 feet, and the starboard bossing was damaged from 11 to 18 feet aft of the hole on its upper surface.

Fig. 8-01 The rent in *Olympic* above the waterline near frame 113.

At the time of the collision a greaser was standing on the fore side of the watertight door in bulkhead "O" in the aftermost section of the tunnel compartment that was located just aft of *Olympic*'s electric dynamos room. At the moment *Hawke* struck, he saw *Hawke*'s ram penetrate into *Olympic* and, as *Hawke* drifted out, he saw water come in with a rush. During that time, the automatic watertight door release from the bridge had not yet been worked, and the greaser grabbed the watertight door hand lever and manually released the door which dropped shut as it was designed to do. However, during the time it took to do so, sufficient water had come through the door to bring about 3 feet of water into the shaft tunnel compartment ahead of the bulkhead – some 300 or 400 tons. The door closed, and the water was subsequently pumped out. Meanwhile, the tunnel compartment aft of bulkhead "O" was completely flooded, and the vessel trimmed down a bit by the stern.

Fig. 8-02 **The flooding on *Olympic* immediately following the collision.**

It was clear that extensive and expensive repairs would be needed to make *Olympic* ready for sea again. *Olympic* had anchored overnight in Osbourne Bay, and shortly after 8am the following day there were six tugs attending to her (two on each side and then two at the bow). They towed her slowly into port as passengers watched from the upper decks. By 10:30am, she was at the dock entrance, and it then took another fifteen minutes until she was safely berthed, her stern lower in the water than usual due to the flooded compartment.

On 23 September 1911, it was reported that the White Star Line was going to arrange for temporary repairs to be carried out to *Olympic* so that she could return to Belfast for a full survey and repairs. It was only at Harland & Wolff's Belfast yard that she could be dry docked because there was no facility anywhere else in the world that could accommodate her immense hull.

A partial survey had already revealed:

> On starboard quarter at break of poop, a large triangular hole about 12 feet in length at upper part fore and aft, and extending from just above waterline to D deck, a height of about 14 feet. The shell plating is crushed and bent inwards for a distance of about 8 feet, also deck plating, beams and frames in vicinity of same broken and started; cabin bulkheads and fittings in wake damaged. The shell plating from the large hole is scored slightly for a distance of about 60 feet aft. It is at present anticipated that eight bottom plates will require renewal and three removed faired and replaced, but this may require modification on opening out. The stuffing box bulkhead, and gland to starboard shaft is

strained, and water finding its way through fittings into the dynamo room, but temporary measures have been taken to stop leak as much as possible.

Divers employed by the White Star company report that there is a large pear shaped hole in shell plating below water, and immediately under the large hole previously referred to, and this was apparently caused by point of ram of HMS *Hawke*. Also the [propeller shaft] boss plating around starboard shaft badly strained for a distance of about 12 to 14 feet; and blades of starboard propeller broken.

The temporary repairs included wooden patching over the hole that was visible above the waterline. *Olympic* left Southampton on 3 October 1911, drawing 29 feet 9 inches at the bow and 30 feet 11 inches at the stern, and she arrived in Belfast on 6 October 1911.

On 14 October 1911, Harland & Wolff reported no signs that the port or centre propellers had been touched or damaged by the collision in any way. On the starboard side, the wing propeller boss was undamaged and the propeller blades needed renewing. They decided to examine thoroughly the high pressure piston and connecting rod of the starboard engine, because the engine had been running at high speed when it had been brought up by the collision. The aftermost section of the propeller shafting needed to be removed and a section of it was bent, but the process was quite tricky:

> The tail shaft can be withdrawn into the dock and so removed to the shop, the three pieces forward of this necessitate that certain plates should be removed from the ship's side so as to pass them out into the dock and so send into the shop.
>
> Where the shafting passes through bulkheads, the plating has had to be cut in order to uncouple and pass the shafting to be removed through the orifice being cut in the ship's side.
>
> It is not expected that these four lengths will be in the shop for another seven or eight days, and so the renewal necessary as regards them is unknown. As a precautionary measure a forging has been ordered for one length of shafting. The shafting is hollow and Messrs. Harland & Wolff do not consider that if any length is bent it can be made serviceable by straightening.
>
> The *Titanic*'s shafting is available if necessary but if used would entail considerable delay in that ship's completion, as the engines are now being put into her.

As well as the damage to *Olympic*'s machinery, the numerous structural repairs needed to be attended to, including replacing damaged framing, plating, rivets and other elements of the hull. A number of the portholes, over several strakes of hull plating, had been broken and needed replacement. To make matters worse, the interior damage was considerable. On D deck alone, the woodwork and fittings from rooms 85 and 89 were broken and damaged, and the "remainder of rooms" between frames 93 to 133 were damaged as well. There was extensive damage to third class stateroom accommodation on E, F and G decks as well.

It did not end with damaged stateroom fittings. The refrigerated cargo space between G deck and the shaft tunnel deck aft was "badly damaged through the effect of the silicate cotton becoming saturated with water;" the litosilo deck covering on D, E, F and G decks "for the extent of deck and shell damage has been destroyed;" and extensive plumbing work was required: a fresh water filling pipe, surgery sink discharge, bath and sink discharge, and numerous other pipes and scuppers that had been destroyed.

Initial fears that the work would take three months proved unfounded. The work was completed by 20 November 1911, two months to the day since the collision.

While *Olympic* was being repaired, the White Star Line had a gap in their express schedule to New York. Two days before the collision, the White Star Line had released their sailing list covering the winter of 1911-12. It showed *Titanic*'s maiden voyage on 20 March 1912. By 11 October 1911, the company had realized that *Titanic* would not be ready in time, and so her maiden voyage was put back to the date of what would have been her second voyage, 10 April 1912. The repairs to *Olympic* diverted considerable labor, parts and materials.

The original 1911 schedule contained the round trips that had to be cancelled:

	Southampton Departure	**New York Departure**
Oceanic	13 September 1911	23 September 1911
Olympic *	**20 September 1911**	**30 September 1911**
Majestic	27 September 1911	7 October 1911
Oceanic	4 October 1911	14 October 1911
Olympic *	**11 October 1911**	**21 October 1911**
Majestic	18 October 1911	28 October 1911
Oceanic	25 October 1911	4 November 1911
Olympic *	**1 November 1911**	**11 November 1911**
Majestic	8 November 1911	18 November 1911
Oceanic	15 November 1911	25 November 1911
Olympic	29 November 1911	9 December 1911

* Denotes the three round trips that *Olympic* missed: the first, which was started and abandoned because of the collision; and the two subsequent ones that were cancelled because she was being repaired.

Oceanic and *Majestic* stayed true largely to the original schedule, although *Majestic*'s round trip leaving Southampton on 8 November 1911 and New York on 18 November 1911 was cancelled. *Olympic*'s round trips were simply removed, leaving some considerable gaps of up to three weeks: none of the White Star Line's express liners left New York between *Oceanic* on 4 November and *Oceanic*, again, on 25 November 1911.

In general, at that time of the year the eastbound passenger traffic was lower than the westbound passenger traffic. Nonetheless, there were some disappointing passenger lists such as *Majestic*'s when she left New York on 28 October 1911 with 228 passengers; there were only 28 in first class. *Olympic*'s passenger carryings were always far stronger and, had she been in service as originally planned, it is safe to say that the White Star Line's ticket sales would have been much healthier. When she did resume her service, she left Southampton (a day late due to fog) on 30 November 1911. She took 1,090 passengers to New York, which compared to the 536 passengers *Oceanic* had taken out on the previous departure; *Olympic* left New York on 9 December 1911 with 1,861 passengers, which contrasted with the 647 passengers *Oceanic* had taken out previously.

The costs incurred by the White Star Line were considerable, including the disruption and assistance to stranded passengers after the cancelled voyage; the cost of temporary repairs, the return to Belfast and the permanent repair work; the loss of earning power while *Olympic* was out of service, losing both the record passengers and revenues from her departure on 20 September 1911 and the subsequent cancelled sailings; and then the legal fees and expenditures from their initial suit in 1911 to the House of Lords appeal three years later.

The damage to *Olympic*, disruption to her schedule, and the knock-on effects on *Titanic*, were bad enough. However, the naval vessel was also seriously damaged and it would be necessary to spend considerable time and sums of money repairing her.

At the moment *Hawke*'s bow penetrated into *Olympic*, her stem was pulled violently to starboard by *Olympic* which set her forecastle deck over to starboard at its forward end. However, her stem was set back by the collision much more than what it was set over. *Hawke*'s ram was turned about 60 degrees to starboard and had several cuts in its plating from *Olympic*'s starboard wing propeller. The lower part of the ram was missing, the part later recovered from the channel bottom in February 1912.

Fig. 8-03 Damage to *Hawke*'s as seen above the waterline.

As soon as *Hawke* came to a stop about 5 minutes following the collision, a collision mat was put over her stem in the hope of reducing any intake of water in her forward compartments. It was also determined that her jammed helm was no longer jammed, apparently freed by the impact with *Olympic*. About 1:30pm, ahead both was ordered on her engines as she headed for Portsmouth. At 3:00pm a tug came alongside, and a pilot came aboard to take the vessel into the harbor. By 3:10 she proceeded up harbor, and by 3:50 her engines were stopped again. Within 10 minutes, she was secured alongside the Boat House jetty in Portsmouth. At 6:30pm her crew was given their usual leave while steam pumps were working to pump water out of her forward compartments. At 11:30pm that night, a guard boat was hailed to come alongside. At midnight it was reported that there was a gentle breeze out of the WNW with overcast skies, some broken clouds and passing showers. The temperature at midnight had fallen to 56°F, a drop of 8°F from what it was at noon.

On the day of the accident an initial damage report for *Hawke* was sent from the Admiral Superintendent at the Portsmouth Yard to the Controller of the Navy in London. It read:

> HMS *Hawke* returned to harbour after collision with *Olympic* stem is broken at water line and bow is bent aft roughly about 45 degrees towards Starboard side on a line approximately from stem at waterline to aft side of upper hawse pipes. Plating on port side is torn away from stem and also bent towards Starboard side the fore end of the decks being crumpled upward. Ship is not making water but it understood that there is water as far aft as D bulkhead. This is now being examined. It is arranged unless otherwise directed to dock vessel in No. 12 dock tomorrow afternoon for survey of underwater portion.

By 4am Thursday morning, the watch on deck was already busy cleaning the vessel. At 11:30am tugs came alongside, and at 11:55 *Hawke* cast off from the Boat House jetty and proceeded to North Lock which she entered at 12:08pm. Two hours later, at 2:08pm, *Hawke* left North Lock, and by 2:40pm, she entered No. 12 Dock where initial inspections of her bottom were to be carried out. By 4:28pm all hands were employed in docking the ship and scrubbing her bottom. The usual leave was given at 6:30 that night.

By 4am the next day, Friday, 22 September, the watch on deck was once again employed in cleaning the ship and sweeping up the bottom of the dock. At 10:00am the naval Court of Inquiry commenced on board the vessel. At 12:30pm it adjourned for lunch, and then resumed at 1:35. By 3:35pm, the naval Court of Inquiry was finished, and the usual leave was given to the crew at 4:30pm.

On the same day, 22 September 1911, another report was sent from the Admiral Superintendent at Portsmouth to the Controller of the Navy. This report read:

> With reference to *Hawke* on pumping the water from the dock it became evident that the lower portion of the fore-body had received extensive damage from a cause independent of the previously reported for above water. The ram is bent badly to starboard and the plates of the fore-foot including stem, and vertical keel are torn out of the ship as far back as B bulkhead with clear indications that this was done by the propellers of the Ship [*Olympic*] whilst in motion. Further details will be forwarded as soon as practicable.

Hawke was fitted with a straight stem rather than replacing her ram during her repairs at Portsmouth. She was distinguished as the only member of the *Edgar* class of protected cruisers to be fitted as such. In February 1913, *Hawke* joined a training squadron based at Queenstown, Ireland, serving with other *Edgar* class cruisers. In August 1914, on the outbreak of the First World War, *Hawke* was part of the 10th Cruiser

Squadron along with *Crescent*, *Edgar*, *Endymion*, *Gibraltar*, *Grafton*, *Royal Arthur*, and *Theseus*. The squadron was operating on blockade duties between the Shetland Islands and Norway. In October 1914, the squadron was deployed further south in the North Sea as part of an effort to stop German warships from attacking a troop convoy coming from Canada. On 15 October 1914, they were on patrol off Aberdeen, deployed in-line abreast at intervals of about 10 miles. At 9:30am *Hawke* stopped to pick up mail from *Endymion*. She then proceeded at 13 knots to regain her station, and was out of sight of the rest of the squadron when a single torpedo from the German submarine U-9 struck her at 10:30. *Hawke* quickly capsized. The remainder of the squadron only realized that something was amiss when no response was received from *Hawke* when the squadron was ordered to retreat at high speed to the northwest. The destroyer *Swift* was dispatched from Scapa Flow to search for *Hawke* and found a raft carrying one officer and twenty-one men, while a boat with 49 other survivors was rescued by a Norwegian steamer. In total, 524 officers and men died, including her captain, Hugh Williams. Only 70 actually managed to survive the sinking.

Chapter IX

CAUSES AND ALTERNATIVES

Samuel Halpern

The direct cause of the collision between *Hawke* and *Olympic* was the result of an adverse hydrodynamic interaction created by two vessels steaming under a cable apart at relatively high speeds in restricted and shallow waters. The vessels were initially on converging courses with *Olympic* heading S59E magnetic [105° T] taking her south of the Ryde Middle, and *Hawke* steaming on a course [091° T] that was almost parallel to a line of three buoys off the entrance to Cowes. Although not officially an overtaking vessel in the sense that she was *not* more than two-points abaft *Hawke*'s beam when she straightened out onto her S59E courseline, *Olympic* was overtaking and passing *Hawke* in the physical sense during those last 3 minutes leading up to the collision.

The forces and turning moments that acted on *Hawke* as a result of being passed by the much larger *Olympic* during the final minute before the collision are now much better understood.[1] Various studies and experiments performed over the years since can be used to give us some insight into the buildup of these forces and turning moments. An example of this can be seen in the normalized data shown in the diagram below (Fig. 9-01) that came out of one such study for the case of a smaller ship being overtaken by a larger ship.[2] In general, the lateral or sway force is characterized by a small initial repulsion, followed by a strong attraction, followed by a very slight repulsion as the larger vessel passes by. The time history of the turning or yaw moment also shows distinct phases beginning with a very slight bow-in turning tendency, followed by a bow-out tendency as the larger ship comes from behind, which then shifts to a bow-in turning tendency as the larger vessel passes ahead.

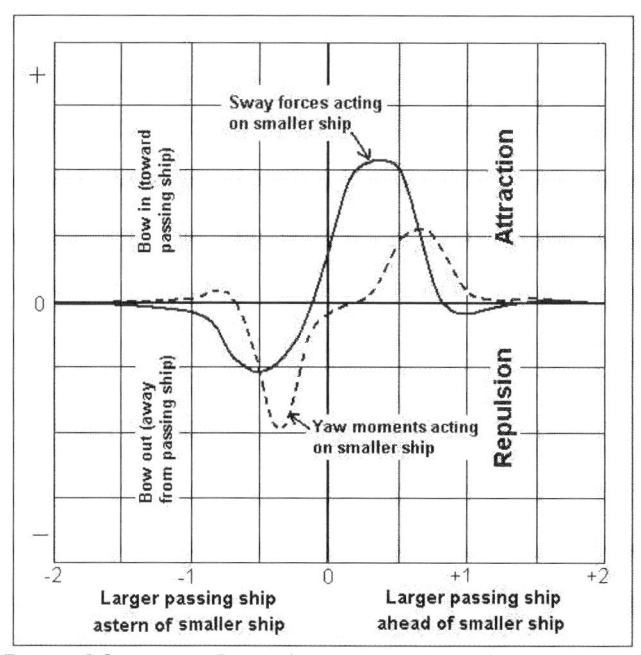

**Fig. 9-01 Lateral forces and turning moments acting on a smaller vessel.
that is overtaken by larger vessel.**

To further complicate matters, *Hawke* and *Olympic* were on slightly converging courses with the lateral distance between them decreasing even after *Hawke* started her turn toward the No Man's Land Fort. From 3 minutes before the collision to 1 minute before the collision, the lateral distance between *Olympic* and *Hawke* decreased from about 2 cables down to about ¾ cables, and the pressure field that was produced became much stronger because of this decreased lateral distance. In addition *Olympic* was still accelerating toward her full ahead speed for channel waters during the final 3 minutes before the collision, and the pressure field strengthened even further in proportion to the square of her speed. Over the last minute prior to the collision, *Olympic* was moving about 4.5 knots faster than *Hawke*. The resulting pressure field was then about 70% stronger than what it would have been had she been steaming at the same speed as *Hawke*.

Olympic's relative large size and displacement, as well as having a relatively full hull form, also contributed to a strong interactive pressure field. Furthermore, the depth of water in the channel where this interaction took place ranged from about 6 to 8 fathoms (36 to 48 feet) as marked on the chart.[3] Taking into account the drafts of the two vessels at the time of the collision (*Olympic* 34 feet; *Hawke* 24.5 feet), and adding 1 fathom (6 feet) more for the state of the tide at the time, we find that there was only about 20 feet of water under the keel of *Olympic* and about 18 feet of water under the keel of *Hawke* when the swerve began. This can be seen in the following diagram (Fig. 9-02) which shows amidships section profiles for each vessel and the variability of the channel bottom over which they steamed shortly before the collision.

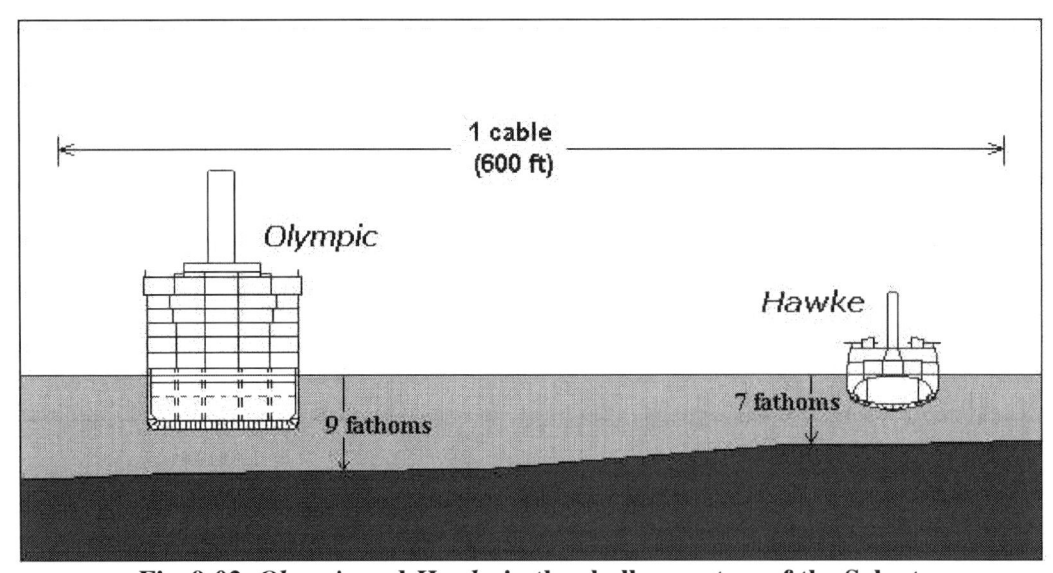

Fig. 9-02 *Olympic* and *Hawke* in the shallow waters of the Solent.

As the smaller of the vessels involved, *Hawke* was greatly affected by the pressure field of the much larger *Olympic*. Any effect on the almost 7 times more massive *Olympic* caused by *Hawke*'s proximity was so small that it was unrecognizable. Being close to the Prince Consort Shoal, there really was no option for *Hawke* to go further southward until she could pass the Prince Consort buoy, the easternmost of the three near the entrance to Cowes. When *Hawke* did take further action to parallel *Olympic*'s course, she started to veer uncontrollably toward *Olympic* as the latter was rapidly getting ahead of her. Once the swerve started, emergency actions were taken by *Hawke* to prevent a collision, including an order for her helm to be put hard-aport (right full rudder) and the stopping and reversing of both her engines. Unfortunately, *Hawke*'s helm had jammed, and the stopping and reversing of her port engine was called into question. But despite this, it is not at all certain that a collision could have been avoided if her helm had not jammed, or if her engines were operated differently.

On the other hand, *Olympic* had some sea room on her port hand side, and she could have gone a little more northward in the channel to give *Hawke* more room. Being on a converging course with *Hawke* on her starboard side, *Olympic*'s initial obligation was to keep clear or slow down. She did neither. Instead, *Olympic* maintained her S59E courseline and accelerated past *Hawke* at a distance of about ½ her own ship length as she approached 20 knots thereby setting up that fatal hydrodynamic interaction. Even after it was seen that *Hawke* was turning toward *Olympic*, no immediate action was taken to avoid a collision. When the order was finally given to swing *Olympic*'s stern away from the oncoming *Hawke*, it was too little and too late.

At the High Court of Justice trial later that year it was concluded that:

1. *Olympic* failed to establish her contention that *Hawke* was an overtaking vessel bound to keep out of the way.
2. The vessels were crossing vessels and it was *Olympic* that should have given way to *Hawke*.
3. *Hawke* was not to blame for what she did or omitted to do.
4. The fault was with *Olympic*'s pilot in allowing his vessel to get dangerously near *Hawke* and not following the established rule of the road for crossing vessels.

The onus was on *Olympic* to prove that *Hawke* was negligent in her actions, and that the swerve that resulted could somehow have been prevented. In the same case in the Court of Appeal, it was held that though it was possible, but not certain, that the collision may have been prevented if the steering gear of *Hawke* had not jammed, it was upon *Olympic* to prove that if the gear had not jammed the collision could have been avoided. This she was unable to do. The ruling of the court was that the collision was caused by the faulty navigation of *Olympic*'s pilot who had admitted that he was not paying much attention to *Hawke* despite the cruiser being within his sight and to which he had previously signaled.

We too cannot find any validating evidence to support *Olympic*'s claim that *Hawke* was at any time an overtaking vessel. In fact, the analysis of the data presented here tends to support much of what *Hawke* had claimed except for underestimating some of the distances between herself and *Olympic* after *Olympic* had completed her turn around the West Bramble buoy. It is also clear that the two vessels were on converging courses of about 15 degrees after *Olympic* steadied onto her S59E courseline with *Hawke* already established on a line close to, and essentially paralleling, the three buoys near the entrance to Cowes. Based on time, speed, and course information, *Olympic* had to have had *Hawke* broad on her starboard bow at the time she actually steadied on S59E, not one-quarter mile aft on her starboard quarter as claimed.

What is troubling to us is the number of officers and others who testified for *Olympic* and said they saw *Hawke* come up from 2 to 3 points on *Olympic*'s starboard quarter from ¼ mile back on a parallel course separated about 300 yards from that of *Olympic*.[4] This was immediately after *Olympic* had steadied on her S59E courseline after turning the West Bramble buoy. It was as if all these eyewitnesses on board *Olympic*, who last took notice of *Hawke* just before *Olympic* commenced turning around West Bramble buoy, suddenly decided to look aft at the same time to get a glimpse of where the cruiser was after *Olympic*'s 11 point turn was completed. As noted in the court findings by the court president, Samuel Evans, "There was an extraordinary similarity, amounting almost to complete identity, about their [*Olympic*'s] evidence."

Even Col. White, a first class passenger on *Olympic* who crossed over to the starboard side of *Olympic*'s Promenade deck when he heard the two whistle blasts, said he was watching *Hawke* from that time until she appeared to have starboarded her helm and strike *Olympic* at what appeared to be a right angle blow. His details of where *Hawke* was, both distance, bearing and relative speed, at the time *Olympic* steadied on her course after rounding the West Bramble buoy, as well as what followed, were almost identical to that given by *Olympic*'s officers. What was strikingly different, however, was where White placed the point of collision, which was about ½ mile beyond where Captain Smith placed the point of collision. Interestingly, Col. White's collision point, which was almost due north true of Old Castle Point, is only about 2 cables beyond where we believe the collision actually took place.

Forensically, we cannot find support for the claim that *Hawke* was at anytime an overtaking vessel. Other observations by a large body of witnesses, including some from *Hawke*, had the impression that *Hawke* and *Olympic* were on parallel courses for several minutes before *Hawke* swerved into *Olympic*. According to *Olympic*'s pilot, *Hawke* ported (turned right) from her S74E course to parallel that of *Olympic* as she came up on *Olympic*'s quarter after *Olympic* steadied on her S59E courseline. According to *Hawke*'s navigation officer, *Olympic* assumed roughly a parallel course to *Hawke* as *Hawke* was passing the chequered buoy on a S74E courseline. As already pointed out, our analysis shows that the two vessels were close to running parallel to each other only after *Hawke* turned for the No Man's Land Fort after passing the Prince Consort buoy (the easternmost of the three by the entrance to Cowes) about a minute before the collision took place. Careful analysis again shows that impressions formed by eyewitnesses with regard to distances, bearings, ship headings, speed and time cannot by itself be heavily relied upon.

Less troubling are the observations of those witnesses for *Olympic* who were on the shore or aboard a moored vessel near the entrance to Cowes. In some cases, such as the observations of H. J. Lashmar from his yacht *Bellinda*, we find a number of conflicting estimates such as *Hawke* passing about ¼ mile off the East Lepe buoy, with *Hawke* being seen midway between the buoy and shoreline on the Isle of Wight, and with *Hawke* being only 300 yards from the shore when she made her turn around Egypt Point.

In the case of A. F. Masters, who was walking on the Promenade by the Royal Yacht Squadron on West Cowes, when asked how far off the chequered buoy was *Olympic* when he saw her pass the buoy, he answered "About half a mile." Then when asked "off which of these [three] buoys was the *Olympic* when you first saw the *Hawke*?" he replied, "I never took that notice...If I had known there was going to be collision I should have been prepared in every respect." Masters then went on to say, "Only that I see what I did see, the *Olympic* was passing up, and the *Hawke* came along her starboard side and ran into her." This prompted the question, "That is all you saw?" to which he replied, "That is all I saw – the collision was not necessary."

Even the independent observations of Lt. Nixon of the United States Navy came under severe criticism from Naval Constructor D. W. Taylor after Nixon's eyewitness account was published in the US *Naval Institute Proceedings* in late 1911. Taylor was one of several expert witnesses called before the High Court of Justice to testify about the effects of hydrodynamic interactions between passing vessels in restricted waters. Taylor wrote a discussion piece in the US *Naval Institute Proceedings* (Vol. 38, 1912) wherein he said that he was sorry to see Nixon's account published in the previous *Proceedings* that ascribed blame or responsibility to either side. Taylor pointed out that Nixon's account, which we also summarized in the first chapter, was materially in error with regard to what *Olympic*'s people saw and did. Taylor wrote:

> It is well known that no two witnesses will give exactly the same account of even a simple occurrence. Lieutenant Nixon's recollection of the circumstances of the collision is not only opposed to the sworn evidence of a number of officers of the English Navy which was accepted as correct by the court, but is inconsistent in material respects with the facts demonstrated in the court by the strongest possible evidence.

Taylor went on to show that Nixon's account as to where the accident took place was far removed from the place claimed by either *Olympic* or *Hawke*, that the courses he showed for both vessels did not agree with what was claimed by either *Olympic* or *Hawke*, and that his claim that *Hawke* was gaining on *Olympic* when she began to swerve into *Olympic* was at variance with what witnesses for both *Olympic* and *Hawke* had claimed.

Taylor did point out that he agreed with Nixon that the swerve of *Hawke* was caused by "suction," but he was "strongly of the opinion that had the *Hawke* approached *Olympic* in the manner described by him [Nixon] the effect of suction upon her would have produced results very different from those that actually took place." Taylor concluded that the evidence presented by both sides during the trial "seemed to render it practically certain that Lieutenant Nixon's recollections were erroneous."

With regard to the accuracy of observations and estimates of eyewitness, The Right Honourable Sir Samuel Evans, president of the court trial in 1911, seemed to summarize it best in his final judgment statement:

> But general observation as to the distances, bearings, and speeds of two vessels turning at different points, at a considerable distance away, about the same time, and then angling towards each other is difficult and liable to great errors. Evidence of that kind requires to be submitted to a careful test; and tests are available in this case. None of the observers at the time were thinking of any collision, and none of them made observations with reference to any fixed objects or the land or otherwise. They may have made mistakes, and harbored inaccurate impressions.

Unstated was the known practice of lawyers to see to it that witnesses for their side avoid certain pitfalls when being questioned, and if possible, to see to it that they are in accord as to estimates of distances, bearings, positions and times of their observations, and in accord as to orders given and the sequence of events that took place.

Considering the question of blame, we also agree with the court findings in that *Hawke* was not to blame for any actions taken or not taken prior to the accident, except perhaps for the questionable call to stop and reverse the port engine once the hard-aport (right full rudder) helm order was given. Up until the swerve began, *Hawke* had little choice but to remain on her courseline paralleling the line of those three buoys by the entrance to Cowes until she could pass the Prince Consort buoy. It was *Olympic* who had room to go a little more northward in the channel to widen the spacing between herself and the cruiser, and this she did not do. The swerving of *Hawke* into *Olympic* was caused by an adverse hydrodynamic interaction that came about as a result of the relatively high speeds of both vessels in restricted channel waters, their relative proximity to each other that came about as a result of initially being on converging courses, and the relatively shallow channel bottom that they each were passing over. If it were not for this hydrodynamic interaction, the accident would not have happened. This point was also recognized by the court back in 1911, but it still found that *Olympic* should have given way to *Hawke* because the vessels were on crossing courses with *Hawke* on the starboard side of *Olympic*. Therefore, it was the navigation of *Olympic* under compulsory pilotage that set the stage that led to the accident.

---

[1] See Appendix A – Hydrodynamic Forces and Interactions.

[2] Marc Vantorre, Ellada Verzhbitskaya, Erick LaForce, "Model Test Based Foundation of Ship-to-Ship Interaction Forces," *Ship Technology Research*, Vol. 49, 2002.

[3] *Glasgow Evening Citizen*, 19 February 1912. Submitted by George Craig to the Lords of the Admiralty on 20 February 1912.

[4] In addition to Captain Smith and Pilot George Bowyer making such claim, we also have Chief Officer Wilde who was stationed out on the forecastle deck, First Officer William Murdoch who was stationed out on the poop deck, Second Officer Robert Hume who was stationed up in the crow's nest, Fourth Officer David Alexander who was on the forebridge working the engine telegraphs, Fifth Officer Adolphus Tulloch who was stationed on the amidships compass platform, and Sixth Officer Harold Holehouse who was on the forebridge recording events and taking the time from the wheelhouse clock.

Chapter X

INCIDENT AT SOUTHAMPTON

Samuel Halpern

At precisely 12:00 noon, Wednesday the 10th of April 1912, two 675 pound triple-domed steam whistles sounded three times to indicate an immediate departure from Southampton's Ocean Dock berth 44. It was the signal indicating the start of RMS *Titanic*'s maiden voyage. Like her sister ship *Olympic*, *Titanic* was a floating microcosm of Edwardian Britain, preserving the typical social class distinctions that were so prevalent in Britain at that time. No expense was spared in the construction of these two giant liners with the intent of putting them at the forefront of the highly competitive transatlantic passenger trade. They embodied some of the latest technological advances of the period, and were considered as the latest triumph in shipbuilding and engineering. For passengers, they represented the latest development in size, comfort and luxury that was seen so far.

In command of *Titanic* was 62 year old Captain Edward J. Smith. On the navigation bridge along with Captain Smith was Trinity House harbour pilot George W. Bowyer who was assigned to take *Titanic* out from Southampton to the Nab Light Vessel, the departure point for the cross Channel voyage to Cherboug, France. Also on the bridge was 28 year old Joseph Groves Boxhall, *Titanic*'s fourth officer, who was working the engine room telegraphs and logging all the commands that were given. Stationed in the wheelhouse was 29 year old Harold Godfrey Lowe, *Titanic*'s fifth officer, who was by the loud speaking telephones with direct connections to phones on the forecastle, the aft docking bridge, the engine room and the crow's nest.

In charge of moorings on the forecastle head was 39 year old Henry Tingle Wilde who was just brought over from *Olympic* to be chief officer under Captain Smith for *Titanic*'s maiden voyage. Wilde was assisted by 38 year old Second Officer Charles Herbert Lightoller who was overseeing the spring lines there. In charge of mooring lines aft was 39 year old First Officer William McMaster Murdoch who was stationed on the aft docking bridge. Assisting Murdoch was 34 year old Herbert John Pitman, *Titanic*'s third officer, who was passing along instructions coming from the forebridge. Murdoch was *Titanic's* chief officer just two days before. Now with Wilde on board, Murdock was forced to step down to the position of first officer, and Charles Lightoller, who had been *Titanic's* first officer when he first joined the ship, was forced to step down to the position of second officer. As a result of this reshuffling of senior officers, 37 year old David Blair, who had been *Titanic*'s Second Officer during her trials and on the crossing from Belfast to Southampton, was forced to leave the ship.

Stationed at the aft port-side gangway down on E deck was 28 year old James Paul Moody, *Titanic*'s sixth officer, who was supervising its withdrawal. He was later to man the standard compass platform located amidships after *Titanic* left the dock.

Down in the reciprocating engine room, 50 year old Chief Engineer Joseph Bell was standing on the bottom platform, called the starting platform, overseeing all operations below in the machinery spaces. Along with Bell on the starting platform was 39 year old Senior Second Engineer William Edward Farquharson who would be working the controls for one engine, and 38 year old Junior Second Engineer Norman Harrison who would be working the controls for the other engine. In addition, there were two junior engineers stationed at the engine telegraphs located on the forward low-pressure cylinder columns of the giant reciprocating engines, and another junior engineer ready to take the time and log all the orders received from the bridge.

Leaving the dock at Southampton was not without incident. After casting off her mooring lines, the 46,300 GRT triple-screw passenger liner was moved away from the Ocean Dock wharf and into the river Test with the help of tugboats *Albert Edward*, *Ajax*, *Hector*, *Hercules*, *Neptune*, and *Vulcan*. Then "Slow-ahead" was telegraphed down to the engine room, and her two reciprocation engines started to work up to a speed of 30 revolutions per minute which would move the vessel out at a speed of about 8 to 9 knots. As *Titanic* gathered speed in those restricted waters, an adverse hydrodynamic interaction was set up between her and two steamers that were moored at berth 38 down by the lower Test quays near the juncture of the Test and Itchen rivers. The larger of the two, the 17,300 GRT *Oceanic*, was moored against the quay while the smaller of the two, the 10,500 GRT *New York*, was moored abreast and outboard of the *Oceanic*. The interaction that took place was even more magnified because of the shallowness of the restricted waters that separated *Titanic* from the two moored vessels.

As *Titanic*'s bow approached the sterns of the two vessels, a small repulsive force was set up between the larger and more massive *Titanic* and the two smaller vessels pushing them both up against the quay. Soon the hydrodynamic force turned from one of repulsion to one of heavy attraction as a low pressure area was set up between the advancing ocean liner and the two smaller steamers that were moored alongside the quay. With the attractive force came an induced turning moment that now acted to swing the stern of the two ships outward toward the passing *Titanic*. As *Titanic* approached abreast of them, the attractive force became too much for the mooring lines of *New York* to bear, and to the horror of those nearby, her mooring lines suddenly snapped.

> "As the bows of our ship came about level with those of the *New York*, there came a series of reports like those of a revolver, and on the quay side of the *New York* snaky coils of thick rope flung themselves high in the air and fell backwards among the crowd, which retreated in alarm to escape the flying ropes. We hoped that no one was struck by the ropes, but a sailor next to me was certain he saw a woman carried away to receive attention. And then, to our amazement the *New York* crept towards us, slowly and stealthily, as if drawn by some invisible force which she was powerless to withstand…On the *New York* there was shouting of orders, sailors running to and fro, paying out ropes and putting mats over the side where it seemed likely we should collide; the tug which had a few moments before cast off from the bows of the *Titanic* came up around our stern and passed to the quay side of the *New York*'s stern, made fast to her and started to haul her back with all the force her engines were capable of; but it did not seem that the tug made much impression on the *New York*.

Apart from the serious nature of the accident, it made an irresistibly comic picture to see the huge vessel drifting down the dock with a snorting tug at its heels, for all the world like a small boy dragging a diminutive puppy down the road with its teeth locked on a piece of rope, its feet splayed out, its head and body shaking from side to side in the effort to get every ounce of its weight used to the best advantage. At first all appearance showed that the sterns of the two vessels would collide; but from the stern bridge of the *Titanic* an officer directing operations stopped us dead, the suction ceased, and the *New York* with her tug trailing behind moved obliquely down the dock, her stern gliding along the side of the *Titanic* some few yards away. It gave an extraordinary impression of the absolute helplessness of a big liner in the absence of any motive power to guide her." – Lawrence Beesley, Second Class Passenger, SS *Titanic*.

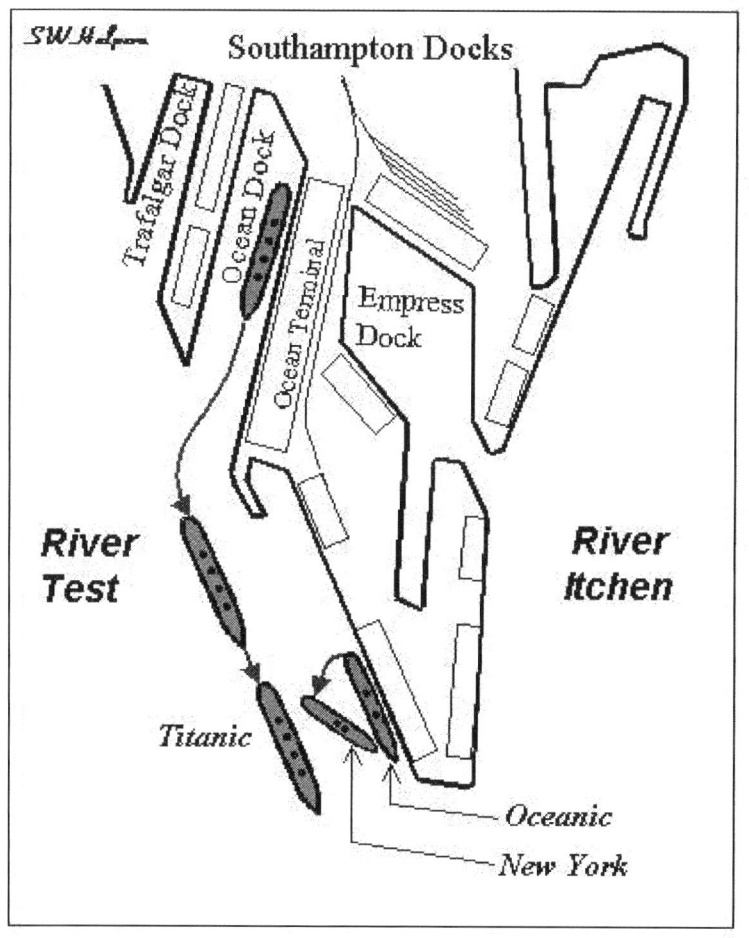

Fig. 10-01 *Titanic* **leaving Southampton Docks.**

The tugs *Neptune* and *Vulcan* caught *New York* and pulled her back toward the quay while *Titanic*, stopped dead in her tracts by reversing her engines for a short time, was slowly drifting backward. But controlling the wayward *New York* was no easy task.

"Someone sang out to me to get up and push the *New York* back, but such a thing was impossible. Had I got between the two ships we would almost certainly have been jammed. Instead, I turned the *Vulcan* around and got a wire rope on the port quarter of the *New York*. Unfortunately, that rope parted, but our men immediately got a second wire on board, and we got hold of the *New York* when she was within four feet of *Titanic*. Our movements were all the more trying because the broken mooring ropes from *New York* were lying in the water, and we stood a good chance of fouling our own propeller. Every rope on the *New York* snapped, the stern lines being the first to go..." – Captain Gale, tugboat *Vulcan*.

Fig. 10-02 *New York* **being pulled away from** *Titanic* **by the tug** *Vulcan*.

The small steamer *New York,* which was tugged about "like a naughty child," was eventually brought under control and moored around the head of the Test docks. It was then that *Titanic* was allowed to proceed once again, her departure from Southampton Docks delayed by more than an hour. Ahead of her were 24 miles of sheltered waters before making the English Channel. But before she could reach the Nab light vessel to drop off the pilot, she had to negotiate the difficult reverse "S" curve between Calshot Spit and the shallow Bramble Bank entering the Solent just north of the Isle of Wight, the same as her older sister had to do on the day of the collision with HMS *Hawke*. As *Titanic* steamed down Southampton Water, the near collision that was witnessed by so many was the topic of almost every conversation. It was generally agreed that this confirmed the suction theory which the British Admiralty first advanced in the courts of law following the *Olympic-Hawke* collision.

Little did those on board know at the time, the collision that almost took place between *Titanic* and *New York* would have been far better than what lay ahead in the ice infested waters of the mid Atlantic that April 1912.

EPILOGUE

Samuel Halpern

Some lessons are hard to learn. In his final Judgment, the President of the Court, Sir Samuel Evans, wrote:

> In the case the speeds of the two vessels were high, and the disparity between displacements of the two vessels was enormous; they were roughly as 7 to 1; and they were in close proximity. Moreover, if the place of collision which I have accepted is substantially the correct one, it happened that just before the swerve the *Hawke* was passing over the shallowest part of a shoal, which would tend to give her a sheer towards deeper water. The *Olympic* was at about the same time passing over a bottom which was irregular and of comparatively small depth…I am of the opinion that in the exceptional conditions which prevailed, the forces set up in the water are sufficient to account for the *Hawke* being carried towards *Olympic* in a swerve which was beyond her control.

Yet not everyone believed in the so called "suction theory" that was advanced at the time by a number of naval experts, including some who testified before the Court. As we have seen, just a few months later, *Olympic*'s sister ship *Titanic* was in a near miss collision with the small steamer *New York* as the new *Titanic* began her maiden voyage from Southampton's Ocean Dock into the river Test. In that case, the hydrodynamic interaction that was set up between the two vessels caused *New York* to snap her mooring lines and swing dangerously close toward *Titanic*. Only the quick action of those in charge of *Titanic* and the heroic actions of several nearby tugs were able to save the day.

But despite this later incident, the danger of ship interactions at close quarters in restricted waterways was slow to be accepted. As late as 18 November 1914, about a month after *Hawke* was lost to a German torpedo, the SS *Comal* of the Mallory Line was drawn against the side of the White Star Liner *Baltic* about 2 miles south of the Narrows in the Ambrose Channel as they were both leaving New York. The *Comal* was on her way to Galveston after leaving her pier at 1:30pm. *Baltic* left her pier at 2:00pm on her way to Liverpool and overhauled *Comal* at 2:43pm. About 10 minutes later, as the ships approached the markers to the channel, *Baltic* sounded two blasts on her whistles indicating that she was going to pass to port. *Comal* acknowledged the signal. Then as *Baltic* passed abeam of *Comal* about 40 yards away, *Comal*'s bow was drawn toward the side of *Baltic* with such force that her rudder could not stop the swerve. *Comal* struck *Baltic* at 2:55pm, and then dropped astern. Both ships then stopped to assess damage.

According to Lt. C. E. Pugh of the United States Navy, who happened to be a passenger on *Comal* at the time:[1]

> It was a clear case of the *Olympic* and the *Hawke* again. The *Baltic* was steaming at a speed of 15 knots, and we were making about 12, and were less than 40 yards from the beam of the *Baltic*, when the suction drew our bow bang into her side.

Comal suffered some slight damage on her port bow above the waterline and had to return to Pier 45 in the North River. *Baltic* lost only some paint on her starboard side and was able to continue with her voyage to Liverpool.

Even today, the dangers of adverse hydrodynamic interaction between vessels continues to be an ongoing concern. Now, after years of study, the general effects of hydrodynamic interactions between maneuvering vessels in narrow channels and shallow waterways is well known. However, the actual behavior of vessels in these restricted waters can still be quite uncertain, requiring a greater level of proficiency in ship handling. As stated by the Committee on Advances in Navigation and Piloting:[2]

> Although there are many texts and professional papers that discuss these [hydrodynamic] forces, their effects, and responses to these effects, there is no "cookbook" solution to piloting. The study of hydrodynamics has advanced considerably, but there is still much to be learned about hydrodynamic effects on vessel maneuvering in restricted shallow water, especially where there are small under-keel clearances. Therefore, considerable observation and practical experience is necessary for shiphandlers to develop an appreciation for the forces and to develop the capabilities to appropriately respond to their effects.

Thus we see that there are still lessons to be learned. With advances in technology, hydrodynamic interactions between vessels can be programmed into full mission shipboard bridge simulators capable of presenting a total shipboard bridge operational situation. With the capability to practice advanced maneuvering in restricted waterways where ship-to-ship interaction effects are included, shiphandlers can now be trained to recognize the dangers of adverse hydrodynamic interactions, and to help develop the proficiency needed to mitigate some of the dangers and avoid collision.

---

[1] From *The New York Times*, 19 November 1914.
[2] Nation Research Council, *Minding the Helm: Marine Navigation and Piloting*, National Academies Press, 1994.

Appendix A

HYDRODYNAMIC FORCES AND INTERACTIONS

What is behind the so called suction theory that causes an attraction between moving ships in narrow or shallow waterways?

It all starts out with the well known fact that a moving ship cuts a path through the water with the water ahead of it being pushed aside away from the ship, and water astern of the ship rushing back to fill the volume that was occupied by the ship. As a ship moves forward a distance of its own length, it transposes a mass of water equal to its own underwater volume. The weight of this water equals the displacement of the vessel. In the case of *Olympic* or *Titanic*, that displacement amounts to over 52,000 long tons of water that is being pushed aside as the vessel moves along.

In unrestricted waters, the movement of this vast amount of water around a moving vessel can be visualized by a series streamlines as shown in Figure A-01 below.

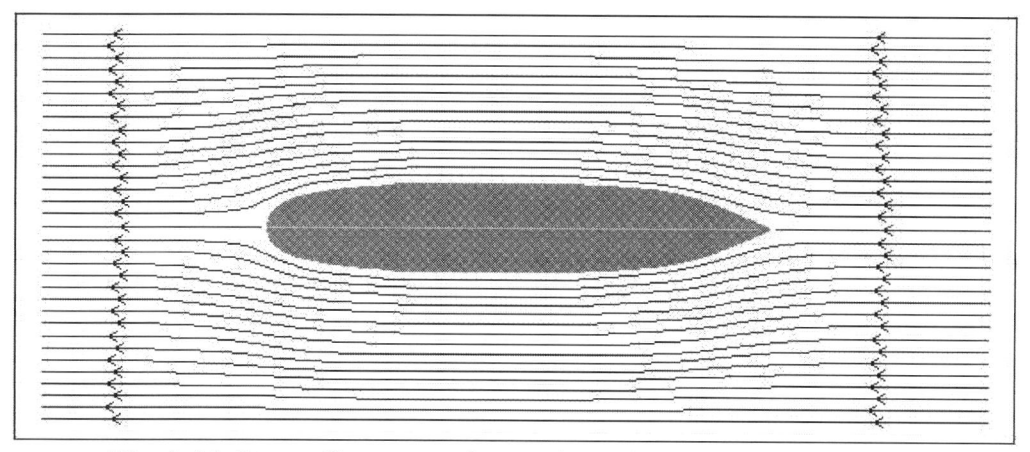

Fig. A-01 Streamlines around a moving ship in unrestricted water.

Any small object floating in the water in the path of this vessel will follow the movement of water along the path of one of these streamlines. It is obvious that the closer to the centerline of the moving vessel, the more an object will be affected by the water flow as it is forced around the vessel.

The pressure of the water also changes in the vicinity of a moving vessel because of two established scientific principles: the Equation of Continuity and Bernouilli's Equation.

The Equation of Continuity states that at any point in a continuous flowing stream of an incompressible fluid (such as water), the speed of the fluid flowing past a constricted area must increase to allow the same volume of liquid to flow past in a given interval of time. (See Appendix B for a simplified example for a vessel moving alongside a quay.)

Bernouilli's Equation is really a statement of the law of conservation of energy. It states that the net change of energy of a fluid is equal to the sum of the change of its kinetic and potential energies. The potential energy of the fluid is proportional the height of the fluid relative to some reference point such as the bottom of a channel. For a given height, the potential energy in the fluid is the same. However, the kinetic energy of the fluid is proportional to square of the fluid's velocity, and for a given height above the bottom, Bernouilli's Equation leads to the well know fact that if the velocity of a fluid at a certain height increases, the static pressure of the fluid at that height must decrease, and vise versa.

Combining these principles, we find that for a ship moving in *unrestricted* waters the ship is accompanied by an increased pressure field at its bow and at its stern, and reduced pressure fields along its sides as shown in Figure A-02 below. The strength of these pressure fields vary approximately as the square of the ship's speed and fade out inversely with distance from the ship.

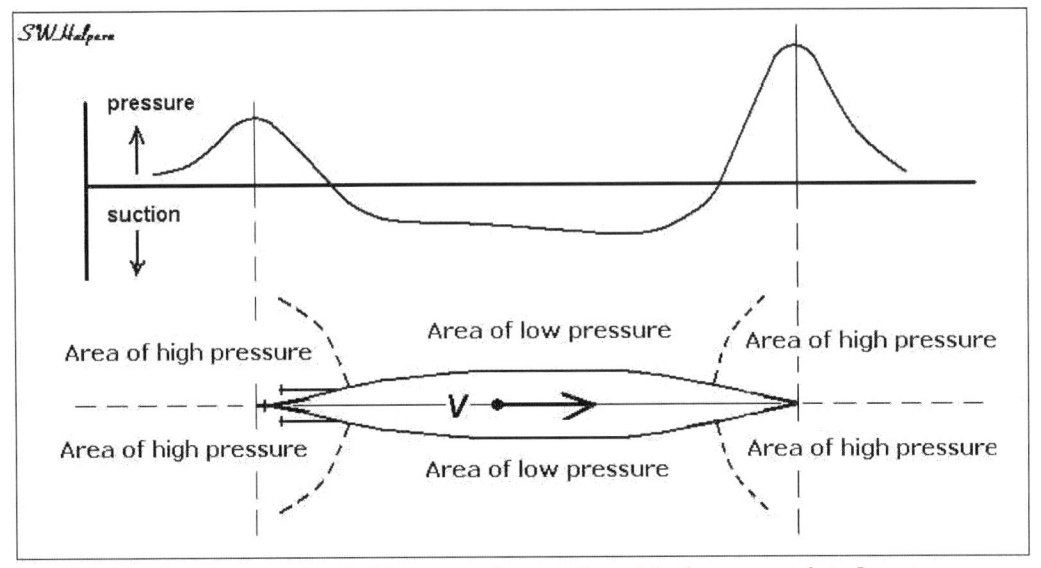

Fig. A-02 Pressure fields around a moving ship in unrestricted water.

In the case of a steam powered vessel, the propellers near the stern further modify the water flow by pushing vast amounts of water astern of the vessel. The cavity created by this action must therefore be filled by an inflow of water coming from the sides and bottom creating an area of greater suction near the after part of the vessel that will affect anything floating nearby. In confined waters, such as in narrow channels and shallow waterways, the flow of water around the moving vessel is further modified by the proximity of nearby banks and shallow bottoms.

The effect of shallow water upon a moving vessel is the creation of a vertical force acting on the vessel that produces some sinkage and trim by the stern. This effect is known by mariners as "squat" and has led to some groundings on sandbanks which normally may have been expected to be several feet below the level of the ship's keel.

The effect of a moving vessel passing close to another vessel or passing close to a bank will be an attraction toward the other vessel or bank because of reduced pressure created by the restricted waterway that exists between the two vessels or between the vessel and the bank. This affect is know by mariners as "smelling the bank" and can have a significant effect on any moored vessel attached to the bank. The curves in Figure A-03 show both the force and turning moment acting on a moored vessel as another vessel passes by at a given speed coming up from astern.[1] (In the example shown, both vessels are of length L, and the passing distance is taken at ¼ L.)

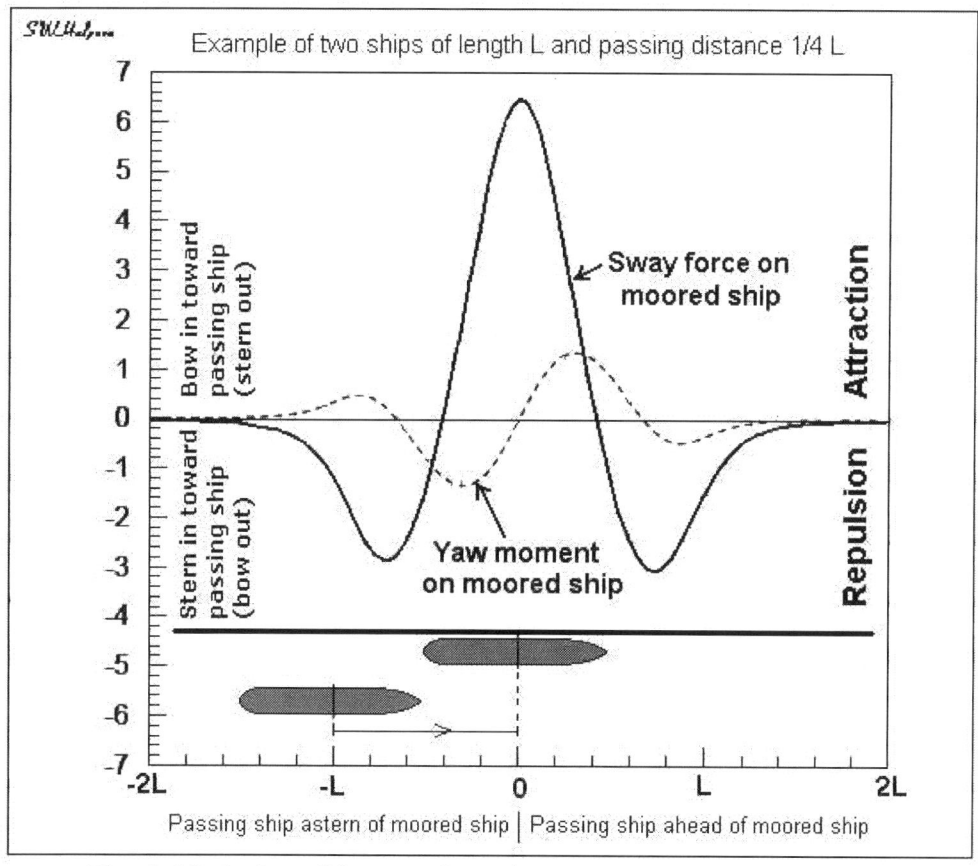

Fig. A-03 Action of force and turning moment on a moored vessel created by a passing vessel.

As these curves show, as the bow of the passing vessel approaches the line of the stern of the moored vessel there is a force of repulsion acting that tends to push the moored vessel against the quay along with an initial turning moment on the moored vessel that wants to swing its stern away from the oncoming vessel. However, these conditions do not last very long, and soon the turning moment reverses, and the moored ship wants to swing its stern toward the passing ship, and what was at first a force of repulsion between the vessels rapidly changes to a much greater force of attraction. This force of attraction reaches a peak when the two vessels are bow-to-bow, and the turning moment on the moored vessel reaches zero. Then as the passing vessel continues ahead, the attractive force decreases until it becomes a repulsive force which soon disappears after the stern of passing vessel goes well beyond the line of the bow of the moored vessel. Notice also that the turning moment also changes from bow-in to bow-out as the passing vessel goes by.

We can now see why the steamer *New York* first snapped her aft mooring lines as the much more massive *Titanic* was passing her that Wednesday afternoon, 10 April 1912. Shown in Figure A-04 are the direction of the forces and turning moments acting on *New York* soon after *Titanic*'s bow swept past. These quickly built up to the point where *New York*'s mooring lines could no longer hold, and *New York*'s stern swung out toward the passing *Titanic* nearly resulting in an accident.

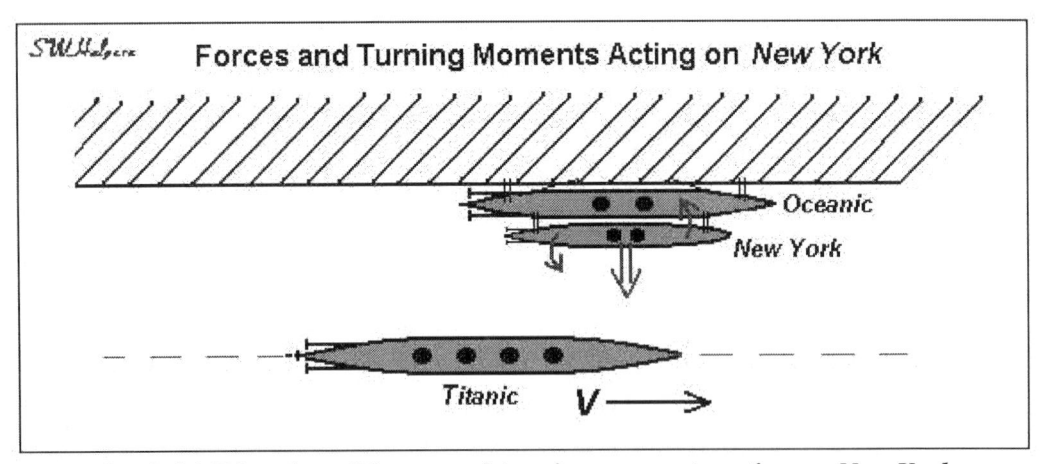

Fig. A-04 Direction of forces and turning moments acting on *New York*.

The basic principles that have been learned with regard to hydrodynamic interaction between moving vessels are:

- The size and intensity of the pressure field produced by a moving vessel is in proportion to the size and displacement of the vessel.
- A moving vessel produces a positive pressure peak at the bow, a reduced pressure over the bulk of the hull, and another but smaller positive pressure peak at the stern.
- The intensity of the pressure field increases in proportion to the square of the speed of the vessel.
- The intensity of the pressure field tends to fall off more or less linearly with distance away from the moving vessel.
- The fuller the form of a vessel, the greater the intensity of the pressure field for a given speed.[2]
- A smaller vessel is always more affected by the pressure field of a larger vessel than the other way around.
- When vessels are in relatively close proximity to each other, the resulting restriction of water flow magnifies any local changes in velocity normally present and therefore increases these proximity effects.
- Interactive effects between vessels are predominant in the region of vessel overlap.
- Overtaking maneuvers are more dangerous than head-to-head passing maneuvers because they take much longer and allow more time for these hydrodynamic effects to develop.
- As one vessel passes another, the direction of yawing moments will change, and the helm being carried needs to compensate for this.

Although the encounter between *Titanic* and *New York* by the lower Test quays in April 1912 almost resulted in a collision, this hydrodynamic interaction between vessels in restricted waters played a major role in the collision between HMS *Hawke* and *Titanic*'s sister ship RMS *Olympic* that occurred back in September 1911.

[1] Renato Skejic and Odd M. Faltinsen, "A Unified Seakeeping and Maneuvering Analysis of Two Interacting Ships," Proceedings of the 2nd International Conference on Marine Research and Transportation, 2007.

[2] The fullness of a vessel is represented by its Block Coefficient. The Block Coefficient (Cb) is the ratio of the immersed volume of a vessel at a certain load condition to the product of its immersed draft, length, and beam at that condition. *Olympic* and *Titanic* had a block coefficient of 0.684 at a draught of 34 feet 7 inches.

Appendix B

THE EQUATION OF CONTINUITY

Samuel Halpern

In simple terms, the Equation of Continuity states that the volume of an incompressible fluid (such as water) flowing across a given area per unit of time must be constant. The volume of liquid crossing a given area per unit of time is equal to the velocity of the liquid multiplied by the area being crossed. If there is a constriction to the water flow, such as a quay alongside the path of a moving vessel, the body of water between the quay and the vessel is forced to flow across an area of smaller cross section. As a result, the velocity of the water crossing that confined area must increase to keep the volume flow the same as before. Why this is so can seen in the diagrams below for a vessel of breadth **B** and draft **F** moving at a speed V_0 at a distance **D** from its centerline to the quay.

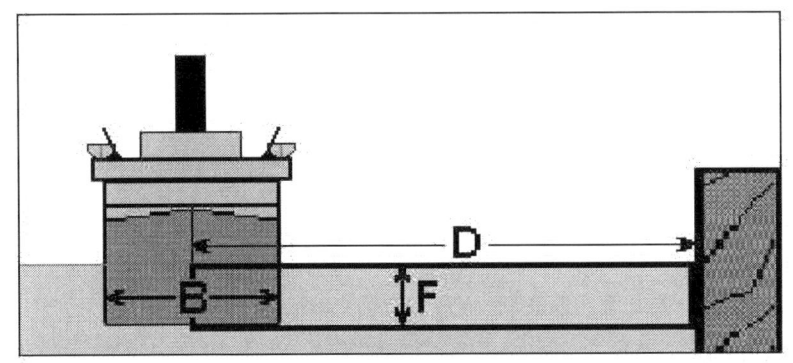

Fig. B-01 Vessel moving alongside quay seen from ahead.

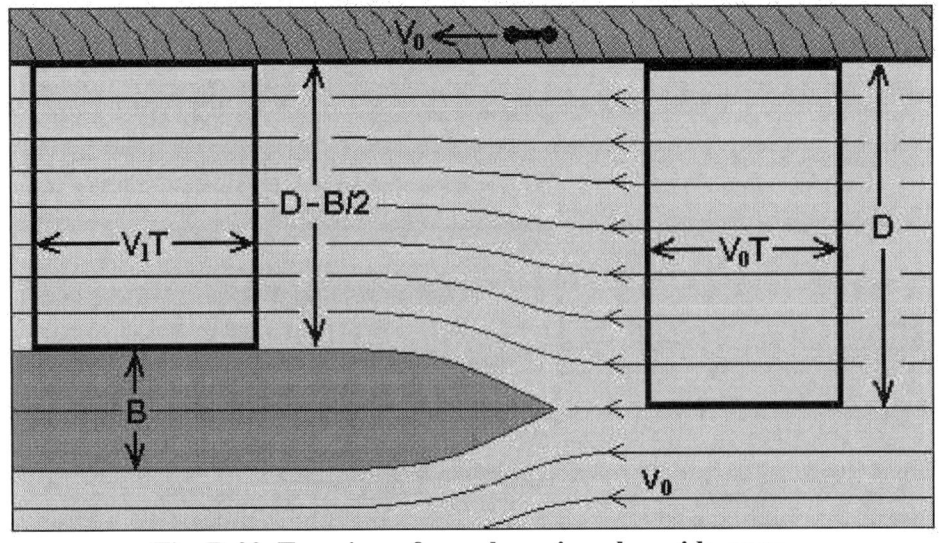

Fig. B-02 Top view of vessel moving alongside quay.

Using the moving vessel as a fixed point of reference, water out ahead of the vessel, as well as the stationary quay, appears to be moving toward the vessel at a rate **V₀**, the speed of the vessel. Over a short period of time **T**, the volume of water that appears to cross an area being swept at some fixed distance well out in front of the vessel, measured between the vessel's centerline and the line of the quay down to the vessel's depth, is equal to **D*F*V₀*T**. However, between the quay and the vessel, that same volume of water must fit between the vessel's side and the quay because water is not compressible. The distance between the vessel's side and the quay is **D - B/2**. Therefore the volume of water crossing an area between the vessel's side and the quay down to the vessel's depth over the same time period **T** must equal **(D - B/2)*F*V₁*T**, where **V₁** is the velocity of the water as seen from the vessel between the vessel's side and the quay. Since both of these volumes must be the same, we have:

$$D*F*V_0*T = (D - B/2)*F*V_1*T$$

Solving for **V₁**, the apparent velocity of the water between the side of the vessel and the quay as seen from the moving vessel, we get:

$$V_1 = V_0*D/(D - B/2)$$

Using a vessel such as *Olympic* or *Titanic* that has a breadth of B = 92 feet, and moving at a speed of V_0 = 10 knots along the side of a quay that is only D = 275 feet from the ship's centerline, we find that the speed of the water rushing past the side of the ship nearest the quay as seen from the ship is V_1 = 12 knots. That is a speed of 2 knots faster than the speed of the ship itself.

To someone standing on the quay and looking down at the water between the vessel and the quay, they would see water moving past the quay in a direction opposite to that of the moving vessel as the vessel passes by. The speed of this water moving aft appears to be 2 knots as seen by the person standing on the quay. To someone standing on the side of the moving ship, the water seems to be sweeping past him at 12 knots while the quay is sweeping by at 10 knots.

ACKNOWLEDGEMENTS

We would like to acknowledge a number of individuals for their support and assistance in helping make this work possible.

Samuel Halpern: First and foremost I would like to thank my colleague and co-author Mark Chirnside for his encouragement, patience and continuous support over the last few years. What started out as something of special interest to me has evolved into a joint effort that could not have happened without the specific resources, insight and knowledge that Mark has brought to this project. I would also like to thank Captain Charles Weeks, Professor Emeritus in Marine Transportation at the Maine Maritime Academy, for his constructive review and support.

Mark Chirnside: I owe a debt of thanks to my parents, friends and family for their encouragement and support. My father's assistance in scanning hundreds of pages of documentation into a suitable electronic format was invaluable. I am also grateful to Ioannis Georgiou, Daniel Klistorner and Gunter Babler for helping me with some of the details of *Olympic*'s schedule in 1911. Samuel Halpern drove the analysis behind this monograph forward and deserves full credit for leading on this project and making it a reality. Any errors are, of course, entirely my own responsibility.

INDEX

Aberdeen (Scotland): 90.
Adur (steam tug): 36.
Ajax (steam tug): 98.
Albert Edward (steam tug): 98.
Alexander, Fourth Officer David (RMS *Olympic*): 12, 47, 96.
Ambrose Channel: 21, 101.
Andrea Doria, SS: 65, 82.
Article 19 – Regulations for Preventing Collisions at Sea: 25, 28, 62.
Article 22 – Regulations for Preventing Collisions at Sea: 62.
Article 23 – Regulations for Preventing Collisions at Sea: 62.
Article 24 – Regulations for Preventing Collisions at Sea: 28, 33, 39, 51, 62.
Article 27 – Regulations for Preventing Collisions at Sea: 62, 63.
Article 28 – Regulations for Preventing Collisions at Sea: 51, 62-63.
Article 29 – Regulations for Preventing Collisions at Sea: 51, 52, 62-63.
Aspinall, Mr. Butler (KC): 27, 30-33, 35-38.
Asquith, Prime Minister Herbert: 27.
Aurania, RMS: 10.
Aylen, Lt. Reginald (HMS *Hawke*): 13-15, 17, 24-25, 28-29, 31, 40, 42-45, 54-56, 59, 61-63, 66-68, 70, 74, 82.
Baltic, RMS: 101-102.
Bashford, Lt. Geoffery (HMS *Hawke*): 15, 18, 23-26, 31, 55, 58-59.
Bateson, Mr. A D (KC): 27, 35, 38.
Beesley, Lawrence (2nd class passenger RMS *Titanic*): 98-99.
Belfast (Ireland): 37, 85-86, 88, 97.
Bell, Chief Engineer Joseph (RMS *Titanic*): 97.
Bellinda (steam yacht): 20-21, 45, 94.
Bernouilli's Equation: 103-104.
Biles, Professor Sir John: 52.
Blackjack buoy: 14, 72-74, 76.
Blair, [former] Second Officer David (RMS *Titanic*): 97.
Blake, Frederick John (WSL superintendent engineer): 37-38.
Blunt, Commander William F (HMS *Hawke*): 13-18, 23-25, 27-29, 31, 35, 39-40, 45, 54-56, 58-59, 62-63, 65-67, 69-70, 75, 79, 82.
Booty, Captain Edward L (HMS *Ariadne*): 23, 25.
Bowyer, George W (Trinity House pilot): 12, 15-17, 29, 39, 42-48, 50, 52-53, 55, 57, 63, 69-70, 73-75, 78, 80, 82, 96-97.
Boxhall, Fourth Officer Joseph (RMS *Titanic*): 97.
Calshot Castle: 14, 72-74.
Calshot Spit: 14, 19, 44, 47-48, 54, 72, 74, 76-77, 100.
Chequered buoy (also referred to as the 'Chequers' buoy): 17, 23, 38, 41, 54, 56-58, 63, 70, 79, 94-95.
Cherbourg (France): 12, 14.
City of Brockton, SS: 10.
Coast Guard station (East Cowes): 21, 66.

Collision sequence: 49-50, 56, 68-69, 79-82.
Collision, point of: 35, 42-44, 60, 65-68, 75-76, 78, 94.
Comal, SS: 101-102.
Committee on Advances in Navigation and Piloting: 102.
Commodore Perry (ferryboat): 10.
Cowes: 13, 15-16, 20-21, 31, 45, 54-55, 59, 66-67, 69, 78-79, 91, 93-96.
Crescent, HMS: 90.
Crichton, Engineer Commander G E A (HMS *Hawke*): 60, 82.
Crookham, Able Bodied Seaman Alfred (HMS *Hawke*): 14, 24, 57.
Darby, Mr. L F C: 27.
Daunt's Rock Light Vessel: 21.
Dryad, HMS: 37.
Dumas, Mr. H C S: 27.
Dunlop, Mr. C Robertson: 27, 35.
East Conical buoy: see Prince Consort buoy.
East Lepe buoy: 20, 45, 94.
Edgar, HMS: 16, 23, 54, 57-59, 63, 70, 79, 89-90.
Egypt Point: 10, 15-16, 18, 20, 28, 45-48, 52-54, 58-60, 63, 66, 69-70, 77-76, 94.
Endymion, HMS: 90.
Equation of Continuity: 103, 108-109.
Evans, Sir Samuel (President of the Probate, Divorce and Admiralty Division): 27, 29, 32-34, 94-95, 101.
Farquharson, Senior Second Engineer William Edward (RMS *Titanic*): 97.
Farwell, Lord Justice George: 35-36.
Fleming, Chief Engineer Robert (RMS *Olympic*): 22, 52, 83.
Fort St. George, SS: 22.
Froude, Robert Edmond (naval engineer): 53.
Gale, Captain (tugboat *Vulcan*): 100.
Gaudion, John (storekeeper Trinity House SE District): 20-21.
General William McCandless (steam tug): 10.
Gibney, Joseph (salvage contractor): 36.
Gibraltar, HMS: 90.
Gilkicker Point: 70.
Grafton, HMS: 90.
Grant, Captain Henry W (HMS *Dryad*): 23, 25.
Gurnard Bay: 45, 77-78.
Gurnard Ledge buoy: 15, 45-46, 54, 59, 69, 77.
Haines, Quartermaster Albert (RMS *Olympic*): 12, 15-16, 56-57, 63, 80, 82.
Haldane, Lord Chancellor Richard: 40.
Harland & Wolff (H&W): 37, 83, 85-86.
Harrison, Junior Second Engineer Norman (RMS *Titanic*): 98.
Hartt (steam tug): 10.
Hawke, HMS: intended courses, 13-17, 59; events logged, 60-61; events timeline, 76; damage sustained, 88-89; war service, 89-90.
Hector (steam tug): 98.
Hercules (steam tug): 98.
Hobart, Lieutenant-Colonel (Territorial Force): 38.

Holehouse, Sixth Officer Harold (RMS *Olympic*): 12, 18, 46, 48, 60, 73, 96.
Horse Sand Fort: 64.
House of Lords: 39, 41, 88.
Hume, Second Officer Robert (RMS *Olympic*): 13, 48, 78, 96.
Hunt, Petty Officer 1st Class Ernest (HMS *Hawke*): 14-15, 18, 24, 58, 79.
Hydrodynamic interaction (see also Suction, theory of): 23, 63, 79, 91, 93, 95-96, 98, 101-103, 106.
International Mercantile Marine (IMM) Company: 72.
Isaacs, Attorney-General Sir Rufus: 27, 35.
Isle of Wight: 10, 12-15, 17, 20, 30-31, 45, 52, 57, 62 66, 94, 100.
Jupiter, HMS: 23.
Itchen river: 99.
Kennedy, Lord Justice William: 35-36, 38-39.
Laing, Mr. F (KC): 27, 29-33, 35-36, 38.
Lashmar, Henry: 20-21, 45, 94.
Lee, George (superintendent Trinity House SE District): 20-21.
Lightoller, Second Officer Charles (RMS *Titanic*): 97.
Lowe, Fifth Officer Harold (RMS *Titanic*): 97.
Maginnis, E J (Portsmouth dockyard constructor): 80.
Majestic, SS: 87.
Martello, SS: 10.
Masters, Albert Frederick (Chief Fishery Officer for the SW District): 20-21, 95.
Mauretania, RMS: 29.
McKenna, Peter (salvage diver): 36.
McKimm, Junior Second Engineer Charles (RMS *Olympic*): 22.
Mesaba, SS: 10.
Moody, Sixth Officer James (RMS *Titanic*): 97.
Moore, Admiral Sir Arthur William (Commander-in-Chief Portsmouth): 23, 25.
Murdoch, First Officer William McMaster (RMS *Olympic/Titanic*): 13, 29, 47-48, 96-97.
Nab buoy: 13, 32.
Nab Light Vessel: 12, 14, 32, 97, 100.
Narragansett, SS: 10.
Neptune (steam tug): 98-99.
New York, SS: 98-101, 105-106.
New York: 10-12, 21, 37, 87, 101.
Nixon, Lt. W C (US Navy): 19, 95.
No Man's Land Fort: 17, 54, 56-57, 59, 63-64, 68, 70, 77, 79-80, 82, 92, 94.
North Thorn buoy: 15, 44-45, 47-48, 54, 69, 72, 74.
Oceanic Steam Navigation Company: 27.
Oceanic, RMS: 87, 98.
Old Castle Point buoy: 43, 66, 68, 70, 79.
Old Castle Point: 43, 52, 66, 94.
Olympic, RMS: intended courses, 14-17; events logged, 72; events timeline, 74; damage sustained, 84-87; sailing schedule, 87.
Osbourne Bay: 85.
Osprey, HMS: 36.
Parker, Lord Justice Robert: 39.

Peel Bank buoy: 16, 70.
Pitman, Third Officer Herbert (RMS *Titanic*): 97.
Portsmouth: 23, 55, 57, 59, 63, 66, 88-89.
Prince Consort buoy: 17, 20, 42-43, 54-56, 59, 63, 66, 68, 70, 79, 93-94, 96.
Prince Consort Shoal: 24, 54, 63-64, 93.
Pritchard, Captain John (RMS *Mauretania*): 29.
Providence, SS: 10.
Puckpool Battery: 57.
Pugh, Lt. C E (US Navy): 101.
Queenstown (Ireland): 12, 21, 89.
Republic, SS: 10.
River Medina: 52, 66.
Robertson, Lt. McGregor (HMS *Hawke*): 13.
Roscoe, Harry (consulting naval architect): 83.
Royal Arthur, HMS: 90.
Royal Yacht Squadron: 20-21, 95.
Ryde Middle: 14-16, 25, 32, 47, 52, 54-55, 57, 68-70, 78, 80, 91.
Scapa Flow: 90.
Smith, Captain Edward J (RMS *Olympic/Titanic*): 12, 15, 17, 22, 29, 38, 42-45, 47-48, 50, 52-53, 75, 80, 83, 94, 96-97.
Southampton (England): 12, 37-38, 47, 82, 86-87, 97-100.
Southampton Water: 10, 12-14, 20, 25, 54, 57-58, 65, 100.
Southeast (SE) Ryde Middle buoy: 70-71.
Speed, Ruben: 18.
Spitbank Fort: 57, 64, 70.
Spithead: 13, 78.
St Helen's Fort: 64.
Stephens, Mr. D: 27, 35.
Stockholm (MS): 65, 82.
Stokes Bay: 16, 23, 54, 59, 70.
Suction, theory of (see also Hydrodynamic interaction): 10-11, 24, 29, 31, 38, 95, 99-101, 103-104.
Swift, HMS: 90.
Taylor, D W (US naval constructor): 29, 31, 95.
Tenth Cruiser Squadron: 89-90.
Test river: 98, 100-101, 106.
Therle, Senior Second Engineer John H (HMS *Hawke*): 82.
Theseus, HMS: 90.
Thorn Channel: 14-15, 19, 44, 54, 69, 74, 77.
Thorn Knoll buoy: 15, 44-45, 47-48, 52, 54, 60, 72, 74, 77.
Trinity House: 12, 20-21, 97.
Tulloch, Fifth Officer Adolphus (RMS *Olympic*): 13, 16, 46-47, 96.
U-9 (German submarine): 90.
Unit (steam tug): 10.
Vulcan (steam tug): 98-100.
West Bramble buoy: 10, 15-20, 42, 44-45, 48, 50, 52, 54, 57-60, 62-63, 65, 68-70, 72, 74-75, 77-79, 82, 94.

West Conical buoy: 56, 59, 79.
West Ryde Middle buoy: 70-71.
White Star Line (WSL): 8, 20-21, 26-29, 35-36, 39, 42-44, 52, 67, 72, 85, 87-88.
White, Col. Sexton (1st class passenger RMS *Olympic*): 19, 29, 42-43, 69, 94.
Wilde, Chief Officer Henry Tingle (RMS *Olympic/Titanic*): 13, 29, 47-48, 96-97.
Wilding, Edward (H&W naval architect): 37, 83.
Williams, Captain Hugh (HMS *Hawke*): 90.
Williams, Lord Justice Vaughan: 35-36, 38.
Yeates, Leading Seaman Henry (HMS *Hawke*): 14-16, 18, 24, 58.
Young, John D (consulting naval architect): 83.

Printed in Great Britain
by Amazon